Matthew's Story

Based on the Gospel of Matthew

Matthew's Story

Based on the Gospel of Matthew

A Gospel Storyteller Series Book

Dr. Marvin G. Baker

Baker Trittin Press
Winona Lake, Indiana

Published by Innovative Christian Publications Division
Baker Trittin Press
P. O. Box 277
Winona Lake, Indiana 46590

Matthew's Story
By Dr. Marvin G. Baker

To order additional copies please call 574-269-6100
or email info@btconcepts.com
http://www.gospelstoryteller.com

Publishers Cataloging- Publication Data
Baker, Marvin G. 1925-
        Matthew's Story/
        Dr. Marvin G. Baker - Winona Lake, Indiana: Baker
Trittin Press

                p. cm.
Library of Congress Control Number:2004094611
        ISBN: 0-9729256-2-7
        1. Juvenile Nonfiction 2. Religion 3. Bible 4. General
        I. Title II. Matthew's Story
JNF049010

Printed in the United States of America
Cover: Paul S. Trittin

Preface

One of the most effective methods for teaching great truths is by telling a story. The Bible is filled with them. Jesus even used them in his ministry. A good storyteller rarely finds it difficult to gain an audience.

A good storyteller stays with the truth but provides vivid details to make it come alive. Facts are vital, but facts alone often do not excite or create a desire to hear more. For example, David killed Goliath. That is a fact, but it could very well leave you with a "so what" attitude. That is not a satisfactory learning experience.

The Bible is a history of actions and consequences. That is one kind of story, historical happenings, from which we may gather information about how to repeat or avoid the same results. The Bible also includes stories that disclose what will happen if certain events are allowed to occur. Those are warnings. These are the two kinds of stories that can directly help each of us to understand the best way to live. They are the types used in the Gospels.

I believe individuals who willingly read the Bible sincerely want to understand how the lessons and stories presented can be applied to their lives. Isn't that why you read the Bible? Don't you read the Bible to know God better and to become a better Christian?

The Gospel Storyteller Series was begun to enable children to read, understand, enjoy, and discuss what the Bible has to say. The books in this series are not intended as translations of the Bible. Information about the geography and culture of that day has been included. The conversational style is deliberate. If the reader cannot identify with those on the printed page, they will close the book, leaving it unread!

From years spent in the classroom, I have observed that one of the most frustrating things for a student is the lack of comprehension of what they have read. I have heard countless students read a page and then be unable to explain what they have read or know what it means.

Telling them to "Try reading it again" made little sense to them. Their question, "Why should I keep reading when I don't understand what I've already read?" is a difficult question to answer.

Do you feel the same way sometimes when you read the Bible? You are not alone. The Ethiopian treasurer had problems understanding what he was reading and eagerly accepted the offer for an explanation by Phillip, the disciple.

This book is an effort to help you understand what you are reading even when a disciple is not there to help.

The Storyteller

My story is an old story, and I told it to many people when I was living in Galilee. It is the account of my journey with Jesus. It is a true story about events that really happened. Because they happened, the world has never been the same.

I was called Matthew even though my Jewish name was Levi. I worked for the Roman government as a tax collector, and it was *not* a popular job even then. One day a crowd passed the place where I worked, and I was delighted to discover that Jesus of Nazareth was with them. He was such a popular man. I was truly surprised when he invited me to become one of his followers.

It was a special occasion when Jesus and his disciples came to my house for dinner.

I invited several tax collectors and some other friends to join us. Of course, the religious leaders were shocked to think that Jesus would eat with people like us. They, as well as many others, were angry with any

Jew who worked for the Roman Empire.

They were especially upset because we didn't keep all their rules. Those men thought we were very sinful people, but their opinion didn't matter to Jesus. He made my family and friends feel very comfortable and at ease.

You must understand that not all the Jews became followers of Jesus. I had the special privilege to be chosen as one of his twelve disciples. We became his closest friends. The years I spent with him really changed my life. After he was gone, many of my Jewish friends continued asking about him. That's why I decided to write my story.

I'm a business man and I included some things that other writers might omit. I wanted people to know the family history of Jesus. Devoted Jews were certainly proud when they could trace their ancestors all the way back to Abraham. I wanted them to understand that Jesus truly was the Messiah.

Matthew

Chapter 1

Some people want proof that what others tell them is really true. They have a hard time accepting things they did not personally see or hear. Since Jesus did so many amazing things, many people certainly felt that way about what was told to them about him.

As Jews, we are very proud of our ancestors. Each family keeps its genealogy, a careful record of their ancestors. It is important for you to know the genealogy of Jesus Christ, often called the son of David, the son of Abraham.

This is not a history of the Jewish people, but there are some important things about us you need to know. This will help you better understand how and why we divide our history the way we do.

Abraham and King David were the two most important leaders of our nation. We mark our history by the years they were our leaders.

There were fourteen generations from Abraham to

King David.

Abraham	Father of	Isaac
Isaac	Father of	Jacob
Jacob	Father of	Judah and his brothers
Judah	Father of	Perez and Zerah whose mother was Tamar
Perez	Father of	Hezron
Hezron	Father of	Ram
Ram	Father of	Amminadab
Amminadab	Father of	Nahshon
Nahson	Father of	Salmon
Salmon	Father	Boaz whose mother was Rahab
Boaz	Father of	Obed whose mother was Ruth
Obed	Father of	Jesse
Jesse	Father of	King David

The middle period covered the fourteen generations from King David to the time we were exiled, being forced to move from our home to Babylon which is now called Iraq.

David	Father of	Solomon whose mother had been the wife of Uriah
Solomon	Father of	Rehoboam
Rehoboam	Father of	Abijah
Abijah	Father of	Asa
Asa	Father of	Jehoshaphat
Jehoshaphat	Father of	Jehoram
Jehoram	Father of	Uzziah
Uzziah	Father of	Jotham
Jotham	Father of	Ahaz
Ahaz	Father of	Hezekiah
Hezekiah	Father of	Manasseh
Manasseh	Father of	Amon
Amon	Father of	Josiah
Josiah	Father of	Jeconiah and his brothers at the time of the exile to Babylon

The third period of our history covered the fourteen generations following our exile to Babylon. It ended with the most important event of all time, the birth of Jesus Christ.

Jeconiah	Father of	Shealtiel
Shealtiel	Father of	Zerubbabel
Zerubbabel	Father of	Abiud
Abiud	Father of	Eliakim
Eliakim	Father of	Azor
Azor	Father of	Zadok
Zadok	Father of	Akim
Akim	Father of	Eliud
Eliud	Father of	Eleazar
Eleazar	Father of	Matthan
Matthan	Father of	Jacob
Jacob	Father of	Joseph
Joseph	Husband of Mary the mother of Jesus who is called Christ. Few people knew that Joseph was not the father of Jesus.	

My story begins several months before the birth of Jesus, the Christ.

In order to understand this entire story, you need to know our custom about people who get engaged. As soon as it happens, we begin referring to them as husband and wife. If the couple changes their minds and decide not to get married, they have to get a divorce signed by their families. Now, all that may seem a little mixed up, but it helps to explain what happened in the next few days in the lives of Mary and Joseph.

Joseph, like many other men in Galilee, was an independent businessman, a carpenter. I never asked, but friends thought he was about thirty years old when he became engaged to Mary. From all indications, since so little is known about this man of history, he must have been rather shy. However, he was sufficiently satisfied with his livelihood that he proposed marriage to a young teenage girl, named Mary, and they were engaged to be married.

It has never been disclosed when Joseph first learned Mary was pregnant. We have no account of the agony Mary may have experienced realizing that she had to tell Joseph what had taken place. How do you share this kind of news with the man to whom you are engaged?

It was a shocking announcement to Joseph. With whom do you confide your heartbreak when you don't want to disclose the reason for your misery? What man in the community would be eager to reveal that his fiance was pregnant and he wasn't the father?

Joseph and Mary had not yet been living together, yet she was bearing a child. Nazareth was like any other village. The news about her condition would spread rapidly as soon as it was known.

Joseph knew it was not his child. He felt shame and embarrassment. He knew his neighborhood. People there, like everywhere else, thrive on gossip.

Above all else, he knew God.

Who could condemn his initial reaction to break their engagement? It would be done quietly. Every man has his pride. Joseph knew the law, but he was a prudent man. Over reacting would only make it more difficult for the young girl he loved an intended to mary. He decided to sleep on the news before he acted.

Sleep was difficult that night, actually nearly impossible until he finally fell into a dream

This was no ordinary dream. It focused on his immediate problem. In the dream he was spoken to by an angel who told him, "Joseph, you are a son of David. Don't be afraid to take Mary home as your wife. God's Spirit is the father of her child, and she will have a son. You are to name him Jesus because he will save his people from their sins."

Even in his sleep he recalled the words of the prophet, "A virgin girl shall become pregnant, and she will have a son. They will call him Immanuel which means God with us."

When he awakened, he was at peace. As Mary had been chosen to be the mother of the Christ-child, Joseph, this carpenter, was chosen to be the step-father of the Son of God.

Because he was a devout man, he did exactly what the angel told him to do. He took Mary home as his wife. He didn't understand why or how things could be this way, but God said she was a virgin, having had no sexual contact with any man.

Joseph did not have any sexual contact with Mary until after her son was born. Joseph named the baby Jesus just as God had instructed him.

Months passed and the birth of Jesus created a lot of unexpected excitement.

Chapter 2

A short time before the baby was to be born, Mary and Joseph had to make `the ninety mile trip from their hometown, Nazareth in the country of Galilee, to Bethlehem in country of Judea.

Jesus was born there in Bethlehem. They continued living there just five miles from Jerusalem. This happened while Herod the Great was king of Judea. He served under his friend, the Roman Emperor, Caesar Augustus.

One day a caravan led by three mysterious strangers arrived in Jerusalem. No one was certain how many were in the caravan, but they certainly got a lot of attention. The three leaders were not the usual kind of travelers who came to Jerusalem. The news of their arrival spread quickly. It was not long before the city leaders knew these men were important astronomers from Persia, (now called Iran) a country far to the east of Judea.

The strangers started asking some very unusual and unsettling questions. They asked everyone they met,

"Where is the young child who is born king of the Jews?" People were even more surprised by what else they had to say. "We have come to worship him. Our home is in an eastern country, and as we studied the sky there we saw *his* star. It captured our full attention, and we have traveled this long distance following his star. It stopped over your city, and that is why we are here."

Well, you can imagine what happened. As soon as King Herod heard about this, he was really upset. In fact, he wasn't the only one who felt that way.

"Have you heard the news?" one after another kept asking.

"Did you know the Jews were expecting a new king?"

"It's news to me," was the usual response.

No one seemed to know that a new Jewish king was to be born! What about the government officials from Rome? Did they know? What would they do about this if it proves to be true?

The normal routine in the city was interrupted. Many were disturbed. Change can be so threatening. This is especially true when a powerful empire, like Rome, rules your own small country.

King Herod didn't wait long before he took action. He arranged a meeting with important national leaders. Among those called to his palace were the chief priests, the teachers, and the judges of Jewish law.

"You men have heard the same rumors I've heard," Herod announced. "What can you tell me about all this?"

Herod was visibly annoyed as he questioned his national leaders.

One man nudged the man next to him and quietly asked, "Have you ever seen Herod this nervous?"

"No" he whispered quickly.

"Who has the answer?" Herod shouted. "Do these foreigners know more about what is going on here in my country than any of you?" Before anyone could answer, he asked, "Where is this Messiah, the Christ, supposed to be born?"

How surprising that he, Herod, would call him the Christ. More than one man put that in his memory to think about another day.

The chief priests huddled together and their spokesman answered, "The Messiah is to be born just down the road in Bethlehem here in Judea."

"Have you known this all the time?" Herod asked pointedly.

The chief priest avoided the last question and continued. "Many years ago our prophet, Micah, wrote this prophesy: "Bethlehem, in Judea, will be more important than other places. A ruler would be born there who will be the shepherd of Israel, God's people."

Wow! What a strange turn of events. King Herod, with all his powerful connections with the Roman Empire, was caught off guard. He was on the defensive. Some considered him to be a puppet of Rome, always doing exactly what they wanted. Now this frightful news! A new king was born, and he had to learn about it from strangers

. . . strangers from another country at that. What will happen to him if the story is really true? What will happen to their whole country if Rome finds out?

Herod was a smart politician, and he called one of his most trusted spies. In private Herod said to him, "You heard the discussion. We have to move, and it must be done quickly. Do whatever you have to, but find those astronomers. I want first-hand information, and I want it immediately, but don't let anyone know what you are doing!"

Herod's wishes were actually commands. What Herod wanted, Herod got. If he didn't, someone paid the consequences! So his trusted spy and the few assistants he chose left the palace in search of the foreigners.

Finding them was no problem. Even in a city the size of Jerusalem, it wasn't hard to find a caravan of wealthy strangers. It was obvious to everyone that they were not businessmen on their way to Egypt.

Herod's spy approached the one who seemed to be the leader. "Sir, I am from the palace of our king, Herod the Great. He would be pleased if you and your friends would return with me so he could officially welcome you to our country." The invitation was accepted and they went to Herod's palace.

As soon as they arrived, they were ushered into the presence of the king. "Welcome, most noble guests, to our country and to my humble palace," Herod gushed. The polite words were spoken with more warmth and smiles than you might expect from Herod. He wanted something from these men. He desperately needed information, so he could afford to be generous with his offerings of hospitality.

"I am honored by your presence. If I can . . . in any way . . . make your visit more enjoyable, it would be my privilege to assist." Herod really emphasized the words *in any way.*

"Thank you, your majesty," the leader replied. "We do have a question, and we are eager to have an answer."

"By all means, let me seek the answer for you," Herod graciously offered.

"Your majesty, from our homes far to the east we have followed a star to your wonderful city. We are seeking the child who . . . according to our research . . . has been born king of the Jews. We have come to worship him and present gifts to him."

Herod thought to himself, *This is going better than I expected, but I still need more information.* To the Magi he said, "How interesting that you have been following a star. With your extensive knowledge of the heavens, I am certain you have researched all of this very carefully. Exactly when did the star first appear?" He thought he was really being quite clever.

"Thank you for your complement, your majesty," the visitors looked from one to the other before the leader told Herod when they were first aware of the star. Then he pressed him for an answer. "Sir, we are truly eager to find the young child. Can you tell us where he was born?"

Herod actually seemed willing to help them. "This

19

child, that you say has been born King of the Jews, is in Bethlehem. When you find him, please share the information for I, too, would like to go and worship him."

Herod was filled with mixed emotions. He had tricked them into telling the approximate time when the star first appeared. But he was angry that anyone would be considered a king instead of himself.

The astronomers left the palace with the information they had been looking for. Heading for Bethlehem, they once more saw the star they had seen in the east. It stopped over the house where Mary, Joseph, and Jesus lived.

It was an amazing picture. The astronomers, educated men from the east, were at the simple home of a Galilean carpenter and his wife. The young child was playing when the visitors arrived.

It is difficult to imagine what was going on in the minds of Mary and Joseph. They both knew that Jesus was different from any child ever born. But this? They never expected wealthy men in a caravan from a foreign country would come to see their child. Joseph remembered that the angel had said, "He will save his people from their sins." He still could not imagine what that meant.

When the astronomers knelt before Jesus and worshiped him, Mary and Joseph were in awe. They were equally amazed when the foreigners offered the gifts to their child. There was gold, incense, and myrrh. Such treasures! Mary and Joseph found words inadequate to express their feelings. Soon, the caravan left this modest home in Bethlehem.

The foreigners did not return to Jerusalem for they were warned in a dream not to go back to Herod. They chose another route for their return to Persia.

After the visitors were gone, an angel appeared to Joseph in a dream. "Get up. Take the young child and his mother and escape to Egypt. You must stay there until it is safe to return. Herod is searching for Jesus and wants to kill him."

Joseph wasted no time. He got up, packed their few belongings, and started on the long trip to Egypt with his young family. They stayed in Egypt until Herod the Great died. One more ancient prophecy had come true. Hundreds of years earlier, the prophet Hosea had written that God's son would be called out of Egypt.

When the foreigners did not return to the palace in Jerusalem, Herod was furious. They had tricked him. He had to do something quickly before this situation got out of hand. Once more he talked with some of his most trusted men.

"Here's what we know," Herod announced, "but it's not much to go on. I was able to trick them into telling me when the star first appeared. How many months do you think it took them to get to Jerusalem?" They talked among themselves and gave their answer.

"Well, according to your time table," Herod calculated, "that kid is already more than a year old! In fact, he could be almost two years old. We've got to put an end to this problem, and do it now!"

"Kill all the boys in and around Bethlehem who are younger than two years old." The orders were given, and the men made the five-mile trip to Bethlehem. Going from house to house they carried out the bloody orders. Every boy under the age of two was murdered.

From all parts of the city and the surrounding area the cries were heartbreaking. Many remembered the words of Jeremiah, the prophet. "There was weeping and much sorrow in Ramah. Rachel was weeping for her children. No one could comfort her. She had lost her children forever."

A few months later King Herod died. Once again an angel appeared to Joseph in a dream. "Get up and go back home. Herod the Great is dead."

Joseph did as the angel told him. Gathering their belongings together, they started on the long journey home. When they reached the border of Judea, Joseph heard that Herod's son, Archelaus, was now the king in Judea. He was afraid to go there.

Again warned in a dream, Joseph decided to avoid Judea altogether. They probably traveled north on a road through the Greek cities along the coast of the Mediterranean Sea. After the difficult journey, they reached the land of Galilee and their old home in the village of Nazareth. Centuries earlier it had been written that the king of the Jews would be called a Nazarene. The prophesy was fulfilled.

Chapter 3

Jesus and his family did settle back in Nazareth. It was about twenty-five years later when news traveled throughout the countryside about a man called John the Baptist. He was getting a lot of attention from the people in the southern Jordan River Valley.

Centuries earlier Isaiah prophesied someone would begin preaching in the desert with a different message. That certainly described John all right. He was preaching in the desert instead of a synagogue.

"Get everything ready. The Lord is coming. Do what you can to make him welcome," he declared to all who would listen. "Repent! The Kingdom of Heaven is near."

It seemed surprising that people from the city of Jerusalem would walk the ten or eleven miles winding mountain road that led down to the Jordan River to hear this radical preacher.

He was, in part, a curiosity for his clothes were

made of camel's hair held together by a leather strap tied around his waist. He ate grasshoppers and wild honey. In spite of his oddities, they walked over the mountains to hear him.

He also attracted people from the whole Kingdom of Judea. In fact, people from throughout the entire Jordan River region came to hear him. It didn't matter to John where the people lived. Regardless where they came from, his message was always the same.

"It is time for you to repent! Ask God to forgive your sins," John declared. "You should truly be sorry for your sins. If you confess your sins you should be baptized. Let that be a sign to everyone that you have asked God's forgiveness. Let the water be a sign that you have, indeed, repented and are forgiven."

Even many of the religious leaders came down from Jerusalem to see and hear this 'voice in the wilderness.' They wanted to see and hear for themselves exactly how and what he was preaching. They were in for a shock!

"You snakes," he would say to the Pharisees and Sadducees, the religious leaders. "Who told you to get away from the trouble that is coming?" He wasn't about to give them a chance to reply.

"What evidence do you offer that you are repenting? Oh, I can imagine what you are thinking. You want to brag about being the descendents of Abraham. Let me tell you something. That's not so special. Look around. See all these stones? God could change them into children for Abraham if he wanted to."

24

Then he added a strange statement; "The ax is at the root of the trees. Every tree that does not produce good fruit will be destroyed. It will be chopped down and burned up in a raging fire." He did not explain what he meant. Each person had to figure it out for himself.

Whenever he was confronted by the religious leaders, John would turn to the common people and say, "I baptize you with water if you repent. That's what baptism represents. It stands for repentance. But there are even greater things coming." The crowd stirred for he now had aroused their curiosity.

They listened intently as he continued. "There is a man coming after me that has much more power than I have. Let me tell you, I'm not even good enough to carry his shoes."

He could hear the people whispering, "Do you know anything about this?"

"I certainly didn't. It's news to me. My, oh, my, John is full of surprises."

"One thing is sure. He keeps us entertained," and they chuckled among themselves.

John ignored what they were saying and went right on teaching, "The person who is coming will baptize you with the Spirit of God. He will begin a process of getting rid of all the impure things in your life. It's like burning rubbish. When it happens, there will be some real changes in your lives.

"Do you know what the farmers do when they harvest the grain? It takes real skill. They use a basket to toss the heads of grain into the air. As the wind blows, it separates the grain from the chaff and blows away the chaff. You city people may not understand, but chaff is what holds the grain to the stem of the plant. The farmers only want to save the grain, so they burn the chaff. Sometimes the fires get so big that nothing can put them out!"

At the end of each day's teaching, the crowds would drift away. Many headed back up the mountain to Jerusalem. Others would camp along the river.

Some time later, Jesus walked down from Galilee to the place along the Jordan River where John was teaching. This was not just a short hike on a trail through the woods. Jesus had to walk from the northern mountain village of Nazareth in the Kingdom of Galilee. I don't know the exact location where he found John, but it was probably near the road from Jerusalem. That would be about eighty miles from Nazareth.

When the two men met, they engaged in the normal chit-chat and exchange of information about relatives. Then Jesus got to the point of his coming. "John, I want you to baptize me."

John was completely confused by that request. All along he had been telling the people that someone really powerful was coming. Now here he was. I believe it was the Spirit of God that let John know that Jesus was this special person.

Slowly overcoming his surprise, John challenged, "Jesus, there has to be some mistake! You don't need the baptism I preach. I need to be baptized by you! I need the Spirit of God working in my life. Why are you coming to me?"

"It's okay, John. This is what God wants done. Let's do it now."

"Well, if it's what God wants, let's do it." They headed down into the river and the crowd followed to the river's edge. John was totally unprepared for what was about to take place.

As soon as Jesus came up out of the water, an amazing thing happened. The sky brightened. The Spirit of God came down in the form of a dove and sat on Jesus' shoulder. But that wasn't all. Everyone there heard a voice coming from the sky, and it said, "This is my Son. I love him. I am very happy with him."

The people were too dumbfounded to speak. Some became very excited. Others were really frightened. Without a doubt, seeing this was a once in a life-time experience!

Chapter 4

After the baptism of Jesus, people left the river area to return to their homes. Jesus, however, did not immediately return to Nazareth. Instead, he was led by God's Spirit into the desert. When people say they are led by the Spirit, it means they are doing what they believe God wants them to do.

He may have gone to the desert area up in the hills south of the ancient city of Jericho. While he was in the desert, Jesus went without food for forty days and forty nights. By the end of that time he was really hungry!

Satan, the devil, came and tried to get Jesus to do things that he knew God didn't want him to do. Satan said to him, "If you really are the Son of God, you could tell these stones to become bread, and then you would have plenty of food. You should do that."

"It is written: It takes more than bread for a man to stay alive. He must also live according to what God says," Jesus answered.

Immediately, Satan swept Jesus away to the holy city, Jerusalem. They stood at the top of the tallest tower of the temple. Once again Satan broke the silence, "If you really are the Son of God, you could jump down from here and you wouldn't even get hurt." At that point Satan quoted from the Old Jewish Bible. "God will tell his angels about you, and they will carry you in their hands. You won't even hurt your foot against a stone."

Jesus replied, "It is also written: Do not test God."

Finally, Satan took Jesus to a very high mountain. He showed him the beauty of all the kingdoms in the world. "I will give you all of this on one condition. You must bow down and worship me."

"Satan, get away from me!" Jesus ordered. "It is written: You are to worship the Lord your God. He is the only one you are to serve."

Satan obeyed and left Jesus at once! When he was alone again, angels came and took care of him.

I, Matthew, don't know exactly how, when, or where he was when it happened, but sometime later Jesus got the terrible news that John the Baptist was in prison. When he learned that, he started the long walk back up to Galilee. He returned to Nazareth, his hometown.

It was soon after that when Jesus moved the twenty miles from Nazareth to Capernaum. This beautiful fishing village is at the base of the Zebulun and Naphtali hills at the shore of the Sea of Galilee. The Upper Jordan River comes down out of the northern mountains and empties into the sea between Capernaum and Bethsaida. This creates some of the best fishing in the whole region.

Isaiah, the prophet, centuries earlier had this to say. "This is written to the people in Zebulun and Naphtali which is across the Jordan River in the land of Galilee. You have been living in darkness because you don't know about God. But you have seen a great light . . . the light that comes by knowing about God. This has happened even though you have been living in the shadow of death."

This prophecy was fulfilled when Jesus started teaching in Galilee. He continued to teach the same message . . . God's message . . . just as John the Baptist had taught. "Repent, for God's Kingdom is here." Like John, Jesus wanted the people to be sorry for their sins and to ask God to forgive them.

I don't know how long it was after Jesus moved to Capernaum that this next event happened. But one day as he was walking on the beach near Bethsaida, he saw two fishermen casting a net into the Sea of Galilee. It was Simon Peter and his brother Andrew. "Hey, men, come with me."

They looked at him in surprise as Jesus continued calling to them, "If you will come and follow me, I will teach you how to catch men and women instead of fish."

This much I know. Simon Peter and Andrew left their fishing business and went with Jesus immediately. Lots of men fished along this shore, so I assume some of their friends may have taken charge of their nets.

The three of them walked on further down the beach, and Jesus saw Zebedee and his sons, James and

John, sitting in a boat. They were working on their nets, probably mending them. Jesus stopped close by their boat. "James, John, I can see you are busy, but I have some work to do as well. I'm inviting you two young men to come and travel with me. I want you to be my followers."

It was an invitation they decided they could not turn down. They climbed out of the boat, said goodbye to their father, Zebedee, and headed down the beach with Jesus and the other two fishermen. Zebedee offered no resistance. I often wondered if in spite of his age he wished he could have gone, too. Staying in the fishing business did not keep him from believing in Jesus though.

Jesus didn't have an office staff to keep track of his schedule. He didn't even have an office, but he was certainly busy! It seemed like he was on the road most of the time. He walked all over the Kingdom of Galilee. Wherever he went he did three things:

(1)   He taught in the synagogues, the place where Jews worshipped.

(2)   He preached the good news of God's Kingdom, and

(3)   He healed people.

You should have seen how fast the news about Jesus and what he was doing spread throughout the huge Roman province of Syria. This is the country just north of Galilee. As soon as the word got out, people started bringing their sick friends and relatives to him. There were all kinds of diseases, and some of the people were in great pain. Others were demon-possessed. Some having seizures and even some who were paralyzed were brought to him, too.

He healed them!

Large crowds followed wherever he went. There were people from the Kingdom of Galilee, the Decapolis . . . a kingdom of ten cities, Jerusalem, the Kingdom of Judea, and from the Kingdom of Perea which was across the Jordan River. Jesus was the man to see and hear!

Chapter 5

Whenever Jesus saw the crowds, he knew he had to find a special place where he could teach. Today he wanted plenty of time to share the vitally important information God has given him. The lesson he planned for today was not going to be just a quick talk or a short lesson like he gave sometimes. It was important to him that the people should be as comfortable as possible. He chose a mountainside nearby, and he and the disciples started climbing. It was no surprise to them that the crowd followed.

When they found a good place where he could be easily heard, Jesus motioned for everyone to sit down. The disciples sat nearest to him, but they were all crowded together.

While they were climbing up the mountainside, I'm sure Jesus heard what the people were saying among themselves. He knew their concerns, their problems, and their fears. He was eager to start teaching. In that last minute before starting, he might have heard someone ask, "What are we going to get out of this?"

Whether he heard them or not isn't important, but he started the lesson talking about rewards.

"You are rewarded with happiness when you understand you cannot do good things in your own power. Then, God's unlimited help is available to you.

"You are rewarded with happiness when you are sorry when you lose people you love. Then, God himself will comfort you.

"You are rewarded with happiness when you are content with who you are. Then, God will provide everything you need.

"You are rewarded with happiness when you have an appetite for what's right in God's eyes. Then, God will completely satisfy you with good things.

"You are rewarded with happiness when you care for others. Then, God will see that you are cared for.

"You are rewarded with happiness when your heart and mind are no longer messed up. Then, you can see things like God sees them.

"You are rewarded with happiness when you help everyone to get along without fighting. Then, you really are a part of God's family.

"You are rewarded with happiness when people make you suffer because you are doing things God's way. Then, you will get closer to God so He can protect you.

"You are rewarded with happiness when people pick on you and lie about you because of me. Then, God knows you are living like he wants you to, and that makes people uncomfortable.

"When all this happens, you should be really happy. You will be rewarded forever. You are in good company for they treated the prophets in the Old Bible the very same way."

One of the disciples interrupted with a comment and question. "Jesus, I don't understand why we would ever be persecuted because of you. What can we possibly do that would make people so uncomfortable or angry because of you?"

With an understanding nod, Jesus explained. "You will be the salt of the earth. You will have value as long as you act like salt does. But if salt loses its saltiness, it isn't worth anything. It is impossible to make it salty again. Because it is no longer good for anything, people throw it out, and it gets walked on.

"You are the light of the world. You can't hide a city built on the top of a hill. When you light a lamp, you don't try to hide it under a bowl or in a box. Instead, you set it on a table so that it gives light to the whole room.

"You are supposed to let people see your light. Let it shine brightly in front of everyone. I want people to see the good deeds you do because of me. If they see your good deeds, they may thank God for what you have done."

Jesus did not explain further. He left it to the disciples and the crowd to ponder just how being salt and light might cause them trouble.

He turned his attention to another question. "If we

follow you, do we still have to do what we have been taught in the synagogue?"

"Let me be very clear." Jesus said. "I have not come to destroy the Law of God or the Prophets. I not only came to fulfill both the Law of God and the Prophets, but I also came to make it complete. I am telling you the truth. Until heaven and earth disappear, you can count on this . . . not even the smallest letter or a single line made by a pen will be removed from the Law of God.

"Let me warn you. Anyone who breaks one of these commandments or teaches someone else to break them will be considered the least important in God's Kingdom. But whoever practices and teaches these commands will be called great in God's Kingdom. You want to be a part of God's Kingdom? Then what you do for me must be better than what the Pharisees and the teachers of the Law do for me."

He noticed that many of them were squirming as they tried to get comfortable. He had them stand and stretch. It was an intermission like they had at the stadium events in Capernium. After a few minutes, the crowd settled down quickly because they were all so interested in what he had to say. His teaching always kept them interested.

Before Jesus could get started again, a man in the crowd asked, "How are your teachings different from the Law of God we've always been taught?" Heads nodded and you could hear people whispering. It was very clear that others had the same question in mind.

"That's a good question," Jesus replied. "Today, I want to name six things where you will see important differences."

You could feel the anticipation as they waited for Jesus to begin.

"Number one, murder." Heads nodded indicating this was an important subject. "You were told 'Do not murder, and anyone who does will pay a penalty.' Now listen to what I have to say. If anyone is even angry with someone, he is guilty of murder. If you call a person an idiot, you have to stand trial in front of him in heaven. If you call another person a fool, you are in danger of the fire of hell. The truth is that words hurt and kill just like a knife.

"Keep this in mind when you go to church to give an offering to God. If you remember that you resent someone for what they did to you one time, put your money back in your pocket. Go and make things right with that person. Then come back and give your offering to God.

"In case things are so bad that your enemy is taking you to court, this is what you should do immediately. Make an agreement with him before you get to court. If you wait to settle things in court, you may end up in jail. You may not get out until you have lost everything.

"Number two, adultery." The crowd was obviously less comfortable with this topic. You were told, 'Do not have sexual relations with someone else's wife.' But hear this, if you men even lust for a woman who is married to someone else . . . you know what I mean . . . you have already committed sexual relations in your heart.

"Don't pretend it's easy to live a pure life. At the very moment when you first have a lustful desire, cover your eye. It is better to live with only one eye than to be thrown out on a trash pile. If you lose your hand the first time it threatens to do harm, it's not the end of the world. It is better to lose one part of your body than having your whole body thrown into hell.

"Number three, divorce." The crowd was really quiet. It was easy to see that some were extremely uncomfortable. You were told, 'Anyone who divorces his wife must do it legally. He must give her divorce papers and her legal rights.' But I tell you, if any man divorces his wife except when she is unfaithful to her marriage vows, he makes her an adulterous woman. Anyone who marries that divorced woman commits adultery with another man's wife.

"Number four, oaths which are legally binding promises." You could tell this was less threatening to the people for they visibly relaxed. "You were told, 'Do not break your oath, but keep the oaths you have made to the Lord.' But I tell you, don't swear an oath at all. You can't swear by heaven, that's God's throne. You can't swear by the earth because that belongs to God, too. You can't even swear by your head. You can't really change the color of one hair. Your answers should be either a simple yes or no. If you say any more than that, you can get into trouble.

"Number five, payback. You were told, 'Take an eye in payback for an eye taken from you, and take a tooth for a tooth.' But I tell you, don't get into a struggle with an evil person. If someone slaps you on the right cheek, turn your left cheek toward him. If someone takes you to court and you lose your shirt to him, give him your coat also. If you are forced by someone important and powerful to carry his things for a mile with him, go along with him a second mile. Learn to live generously. Give to those who ask. Don't ignore or turn away those who want to borrow from you.

"Number six, your enemy. You were told, 'Love your neighbor and hate your enemy.' But I tell you, love your enemies. Pray for those who make it difficult for you because you are living the way I want you to live. When you live like I want you to, it shows that you are part of God's family.

"If you love those who love you, why would you deserve a reward? Anyone can do that. If you are only friendly with the people you know, you are no different from the people who don't love me.

"Don't forget that the sun rises for everyone. You don't have to be good to enjoy the sunshine. Thunderstorms pour rain on those who do good things and those who don't do good things. Crops grow regardless of who owns the land.

"I want you to live with others the way God lives with you."

Chapter 6

When Jesus paused, the whispering increased. What he had just told them was truly mind-boggling. It might even be considered radical and definitely extreme. Those in the crowd kept looking at each other. They knew this was very different from the way they were living.

Before Jesus began teaching again, he was addressed by a man nearby.

"Yes, do you have a question?" Jesus asked.

"I do. What you are telling us seems almost impossible to do. How can we possibly live like that?"

"You will need God's help, and you will have it! I am ready to tell you ways that will help you live like God wants you to live." With that comment, he was ready to continue teaching. "There are ten areas where I really want to help you.

"Number one, giving to the needy. Don't show off when you give an offering to help those in need. If you do, God will not give you any reward. Some people go to church

43

and proudly tell everyone how much they're giving. Hypocrites! Phonies! They want people to like them for how much they are giving. That's all the reward they are going to get. When you give to the needy, do it quietly. Your heavenly Father knows what you do and will reward you.

"Number two, prayer. Don't be like phonies when you pray. Phonies want everyone to know they are praying, so they do it in public. Once again, that is all the reward they will get. When you pray, find a quiet place alone and pray to your heavenly Father who is unseen. Of course, he knows when you pray in secret, and he will reward you.

"When you pray, get to the point. Don't just babble on like a show-off. God isn't impressed by long prayers. He already knows what you need before you ever ask him. This is the way you should pray:

"Our Father in heaven, Your name is the greatest name in the whole world. I want you to be in charge of everything here on earth like you are in heaven. Forgive me when I don't live like you want me to. Enable me to forgive those who do bad things to me. Enable me recognize temptation and stay away from it. Deliver me from attacks from the devil.

"That's the way for you to pray. If you forgive others, God will forgive you. But if you don't forgive others, then God won't forgive you.

"Number three, fasting. Don't look sad when you decide to go without food so you can have a special focus on God. Don't look sick to show you're not eating. If you do, that's all the reward you'll get. Look natural. Wash your face. Comb your hair. Only God needs to know that you're fasting. When you do it without telling or showing everybody, you will be rewarded by your heavenly Father.

"Number four, treasures. Don't waste time collecting and hoarding valuable things here on earth. Things in the environment can destroy them. Thieves can break in and steal what you have. Neither of those ever happens in heaven. Therefore, you should store your treasures in heaven. Remember, you will always love the place where you put your treasures.

"Your eyes are the window to your body. If your eyes are open to the possibilities available to you, your life will be filled with light. If your eyes are bad, you will only see the darkness, and your life will be filled with disappointments. If you don't have light, things can get really bad!

"You cannot serve two bosses. When you try, you quickly begin to hate one and love the other. Or you will have one as a favorite while you try to avoid working for the other one. You cannot serve both our heavenly Father and the god of Money.

"Number five, worry. Let me tell you it doesn't do any good to worry . . . not about what you're going to do for a living . . . or how long you're going to live . . . or your meals . . . or your health . . . or your clothes!

"You have seen the birds flying in the air. You've never seen birds planting seeds. They don't plant their food. They don't harvest it either. And they don't store it in barns or birdhouses. God takes care of them. Surely you know that you are more valuable to God than the birds. There's no reason to worry at all. You can't add even one hour to your life.

"There is no reason to worry about the latest fashions. If you want to see something really beautiful, look at the lilies growing in your garden or in the fields. They don't do a single thing to be beautiful. King Solomon, that wise and rich man in the Old Bible, never dressed that good. God covers up dirt with grass that only lasts a little while. Then the grass gets thrown away or burned. Don't you think he will provide what you need to wear? You need more faith. Learn to really trust him.

"Food? Drink? Clothes? People who don't know God worry about those things. Your heavenly Father knows exactly what you need.

"This is what you should be doing instead of worrying about all these things. Go looking for God. Find out what is right in his eyes. If you do, he'll take care of everything else. Don't worry about tomorrow. Tomorrow will take care of itself. Every day has its own problems."

He was half way through his list, and it was time for another stretch.

Chapter 7

The crowd was soon attentive and ready for the next five points Jesus wanted to make. Without comment he continued with the list.

"Number six, judging others. Don't try to be the referee. If you do, you can be certain someone else will be looking to see how well you are playing the game. You will be judged by the very same rules you want to use on others. They will be just as critical of you as you are of them.

"Don't be a phony. You can't solve another person's problem when you have so many of your own. Don't try to tell others what they should do when you don't know what to do yourself. Don't be a hypocrite. Solve your own problems first. Then you'll be prepared to help him with his.

"Don't joke about sacred things. Do not give up what you know is right to be popular. Don't quit doing what is right in order to please other people. If you do, they may walk all over you and ruin your reputation.

"Number seven, getting help. If you want something from God, let him know what it is. You'll never find what you want if you don't look for it. If you want to get in, knock on the door. Let God know you are ready to do something for him.

"If someone asks you for bread, you wouldn't be unkind and give him a stone to eat. If they ask for fish, you wouldn't give them a snake. Here's the point. If you, with all your human weaknesses, know how to treat people, surely you must understand that your Father in heaven is going to give good things to those who ask him.

"You want help? Think about helping and getting help this way. Consider how you want to be treated. Then remember to treat everyone just that same way. That's a short statement of God's Law and what the Prophets wrote.

"Number eight, making choices. Everyone has to make a choice between two roads. The wide gate opens the way to the wide road. The small gate opens the way to the narrow road. Many enter through the wide gate even though they will be destroyed at the end of the road. Only a few will pass through the small gate to the narrow road. But the narrow road is the one that leads to life in God's Kingdom.

"Number nine, be on guard. Watch out for dishonest people. A wolf in sheep's clothes is someone who pretends to be looking out for what's best for you. They really don't care what happens to you in the long run. They are waiting for the chance to get what you have.

"You'll recognize them by what they do. Don't just listen to what they say. Do they act as good as they claim to be? That's the way to tell if they are honest.

"Good trees have good fruit. Trees that have a disease can't produce good fruit. Every tree that doesn't have good fruit is destroyed. You recognize trees by their fruit. You recognize honest people by what they do.

"It's sad, but some people who act religious are even phonies. Just because you know about God doesn't mean you know God or that you will be a part of his Kingdom in heaven. Only those who live the way God wants them to live will be with him in his Kingdom. The phony ones will brag about what they did in God's name. You can count on this. If they didn't live honestly in God's eyes, he will tell them, 'I never knew you. Get away from me you dishonest people. You have done evil things'.

"Number ten, learning from me. If you have heard what I've been telling you and put my teachings into practice, you are like a wise man. He was going to build his house, and he wanted it to last for a long time. He built it on a solid rock foundation. When the storms came and caused a flood, his house was safe because he had his foundation on the solid rock.

"But if you have heard what I've been telling you and you don't put it into practice, you are like a foolish man. He built his house on sand. When the storms came and caused a flood, his house crashed. It was totally lost because he built his house on sand which washed away."

When Jesus finished talking about all these things, the crowd was amazed. He was not like those who usually did the teaching. He taught them with authority like they had never known before.

Chapter 8

After he finished teaching that day, he went down from the mountainside and a large crowd followed him. Among the crowd was a man with leprosy, an incurable disease. He stopped Jesus and knelt in front of him. "Lord, if you are willing, you can heal me and make me clean."

"I am willing," Jesus answered, and he reached out his hand and touched the man. "Be clean!" Immediately the man was cured of his leprosy. Then Jesus said to him, "Don't tell anyone. Go show yourself to the priest. Offer a gift as Moses commanded. That will be a testimony to him."

Jesus walked on to the city of Capernaum where he was staying. When he reached town, a Roman officer came asking for help. "Lord, my servant at home is paralyzed and enduring extreme suffering."

The Jews considered every Roman officer an enemy so they were caught off guard when Jesus said, "I will go and heal him."

The officer expressed his true faith. "Lord, you don't need to do that. I don't deserve to have you come to my home. If you just say the word, my servant will be healed. You see, I have soldiers under my command. All I have to do is tell them what to do and they do it."

When Jesus heard this, he was surprised. In fact, he was astonished at the man's faith. Jesus turned to those following him, "You Israelites *(that was their ancient name)* are the ones who are supposed to know about God, but I tell you the truth. This man has greater faith than I've found in anyone in Israel.

"This man is an example of the outsiders, the non-Jews, who will be coming from all parts of the world. They will be arriving from the east and the west, and they will sit down at the feasts in God's Kingdom right there with your ancestors, Abraham, Isaac and Jacob. I'm sorry, but some who knew about this faith . . . but didn't believe . . . will not be allowed to be at that feast."

Jesus turned and spoke to the Roman officer, "Go! It will happen just like you believed it would." At that very moment his servant was healed.

After that incident, Jesus and the disciples arrived in front of Peter's house. When they went in, they found Peter's mother-in-law sick. She was burning up with a high fever. When Jesus touched her hand, the fever left her. She felt so good that she got up and began to fix supper for them.

By evening the news had spread that Jesus was in town. People knew where he was staying, so it was no surprise when the crowd began showing up at Peter's house. They brought people who were victims of evil spirits that possessed them. Jesus spoke a word, and the evil spirits left. He healed all the sick. This is exactly what the ancient Jewish prophet, Isaiah, said the Messiah would do. Hundreds of years earlier he had written, "He took our sickness. He carried our diseases."

Jesus looked at the size of the crowd that was gathering. "Men," he said to his disciples, "we better leave for the other side of the lake."

However, before they could get away, a religion teacher pleaded, "Teacher, I want to go wherever you go."

"Do you know what you are asking?" Jesus inquired. "Foxes have holes, birds have nests, but I don't have any place to call my own."

Another in the crowd said, "Master, I'd like to go with you, too. Could you wait a couple of days so I can bury my father?"

Jesus refused. "First things first! My business is life, not death. If you follow me, you must pursue life."

Immediately, he and his disciples got into the boat and headed across the lake. Exhausted, Jesus layed down in the bottom of the boat and went to sleep. Before long they were in a terrible storm. It was not unusual for a storm to come up without warning on the Sea of Galilee. The waves crashed against the boat and came over the sides. Overwhelmed by fear, the disciples yelled, "Hey, Jesus! Wake up! We're going to drown if you don't save us."

"What's the matter, guys?" Jesus asked. "Why are you so afraid? You don't have enough faith." He got up and told the winds and waves to calm down. "Be still," he said. Everything was immediately quiet and calm.

"Wow!" The men were shocked. "What kind of man is this? Can you believe that? The winds and the waves did exactly what he told them to do. Even they obey him!"

When they reached shore, they were in the territory of the Gadarenes. Two demon-possessed men who had bullied the community for a long time came out from the cemetery and met Jesus. People were so scared of those two men that they would go out of their way to avoid walking any place near them.

When Jesus got closer to them, the two men began screaming, "You are the Son of God! You're not supposed to be here yet. What do you want with us? Are you here to give us a hard time?"

"If you are going to drive us out," the demons begged, "send us into that herd of pigs over there."

"Go." Jesus issued a simple command and immediately the evil spirits came out of the two men and entered the pigs. There were squeals and screams as the whole herd rushed down the hillside and into the lake. It wasn't long before they were all drowned.

The people responsible for the pigs were frightened and ran to town. "You won't believe what happened!" they announced breathlessly. Then they gave a detailed report of what they had just had seen.

"Oh, by the way," they added, "you know those two

guys who have been causing us so much trouble? Well, you should see them now."

This news had the whole town in an uproar. It was quite a curious crowd that headed out to meet Jesus. "Look, mister," they said, "we've heard what you did to our pigs. We don't understand everything that happened, but we just lost a lot of money because of what you did. "Why don't you just get out of our country and leave us alone?" they begged.

Chapter 9

Jesus stepped into the boat, and we crossed back over to his town, Capernaum. We hardly had time to get out of the boat before the crowd was gathering. A paralyzed man's friends had carried him on a mat. They set him down in front of Jesus, who looked first at the man and then at his friends. "I am truly impressed by your faith." Then to the paralytic he said, "Son, everything is going to be all right. Your sins are forgiven."

The religious teachers close by were furious when they heard what Jesus said. "Such nerve! That was blasphemy! How dare he say such an evil thing? He has no right to forgive sins. Only God can do that, and he's not God!" they complained.

"What are you whispering about over there?" Jesus asked. "Your thoughts are evil. Which is easier to say, 'your sins are forgiven' or 'get up and walk'. I want you to know that I have the authority to do both." He turned to the paralytic and said, "Get up. Pick up your mat and go home."

The crowd was shocked when the man got up, stooped down, picked up his mat, and headed home. The people broke out in praise to God for sending Jesus to do things like this.

As Jesus walked on into town, he saw me at the tax collector's office. I was collecting taxes for the Roman government. Naturally, this made me very unpopular with my own people, the Jews. The Romans allowed me to charge any amount I wanted to. They only wanted me to be sure they got everything that was due them. Everything left over after I paid the required tax to the Roman governor was mine to keep.

It was a good business to be in, and I made a lot of money. I know that's why people hated me so much. They thought I was a cheat and an evil traitor. When Jesus saw me, he walked straight to my desk.

"Matthew, I'd like for you to be one of my disciples. Follow me." Without hesitating, I knew I had to do what he said, so I left my clerks standing there and followed Jesus.

Later he came over to my house for dinner, and he brought his disciples with him. Many people who didn't have very good reputations came and joined us that night. When the Pharisees, the religious leaders, saw this, they were immediately angry with Jesus. After dinner as they were leaving, the Pharisees asked the other disciples, "What kind of an example is your teacher setting by eating with these tax collectors and sinners?"

Jesus heard what they had asked. Slowly he turned to them with a question of his own. "Just who needs a doctor? Certainly it's not healthy people. The sick people are the ones who need a doctor. See if you can figure out what this means: 'I desire mercy, not religion.' I'm here to call the outsiders and give them hope. I want them to understand that God loves them. I'm not here to make you insiders feel good."

Some time later the disciples of John the Baptist came to see Jesus. "Something has been bothering us," they said. "We and the Pharisees fast . . . you know skip a meal or two to have extra time for prayer. Can you explain why your disciples never do that?"

"Well, that's easy to explain," Jesus answered. "When you are at the wedding, you celebrate. You don't let the food go uneaten. You feast and eat all you can. Later you may have to do without, but when the bridegroom is still with you, enjoy the party."

He continued, "If you need to patch an old garment, you don't get new material. If you did, the patch would pull away from the garment and you'd have a bigger tear than before. You need some material that matches the texture, weight, and age of the old piece of clothing. When you men have new wine, you know better than to pour it into old dry and cracked leather wineskins. If you did, the skins would burst because the wine is still fermenting which causes the wineskin to stretch. The old wineskins won't stretch so they would burst and all the wine would be lost . . . spilled out onto the floor. No, you don't do that.

You're smart enough to pour new wine into new wineskins that can stretch!"

While he was explaining this to John's disciples, he was interrupted by an officer of the local Jewish synagogue. "My daughter has just died," he said. "But if you will come and touch her, she will live." Jesus and his disciples got up immediately and went with the officer.

On the way, a woman who had been sick for twelve years touched his robe as he passed through the crowd. She was thinking, *"I know if I can just touch his coat I'll be healed."* Her hand shook as she extended her arm and touched his coat.

Immediately Jesus turned around and looked at her. "It has happened, daughter. Your faith has healed you." The woman was healed from that very moment.

As they walked on, they finally reached the home of the officer. They were met by a crowd of mourners. It was the custom there to have flute players come and play really sad music whenever someone died. Usually a crowd would also gather, and it would get quite noisy when the women cried. Pushing through the crowd, Jesus told them. "Go away. The girl's not dead; she's just asleep."

They stopped crying and laughed at him. "What does he mean she's asleep? He just got here. What does he know?"

Ignoring the comments, Jesus went in and took the girl by the hand and pulled her to her feet. She was alive! The news spread quickly through that entire region.

As Jesus left the officer's house, two blind men

followed him shouting, "Have mercy on us, Son of David!"

When we got to the home where we were staying, the blind men followed us right in the door. Jesus finally gave them his attention and asked, "Do you believe that I am able to do what you're asking?"

"Yes, Lord," they replied.

He touched their eyes, "It will be just like you wanted because you have faith." Their sight was instantly restored.

Then Jesus gave them strong instructions. "Don't tell anyone about this." But they were barely outside the door before they were telling everyone exactly what had happened. The news spread quickly throughout the entire area.

Later as we were leaving the house, a man who could not talk because of an evil spirit was brought to Jesus. As soon as the demon was driven out, the man started talking as if he'd been doing that all his life. The crowd was amazed and said, "Nothing like this ever happened in our country before."

The Pharisees had to make some excuse. "He must have made a deal with the devil. That's how he drives out demons."

Shortly after this, Jesus began to do more traveling. He went to all the towns and villages along the shores of Lake Galilee. He taught in their synagogues. He shared the good news of the Kingdom of God and healed their diseases. He brought comfort to their hurting lives. When he saw the huge crowds that gathered around him, he was heart broken. They were so confused and had no purpose for living. They were like a flock of sheep without a shepherd to care for them and to protect them.

He spoke to his disciples. "Men, there is so much to be done. There are so many spiritually hungry and hurting people, but we don't have enough workers to reach out and help them. I want you to pray that people will go work with you to meet these needs."

Chapter 10

The first answer to that prayer came when he finished choosing his twelve disciples. He sent us to help those needing help. He gave us the authority to drive out evil spirits and to heal the sick and wounded. Here is the list of those first disciples:

Simon (who is called Peter)
Andrew (Peter's brother)
James (son of Zebedee)
John (brother of James)
Philip
Bartholomew
Thomas
Matthew (the tax collector)
James (son of Alphaeus)
Thaddaeus
Simon (the Zealot)
Judas Iscariot (who betrayed him.)

Jesus sent us out with these instructions: "Don't

go to the Gentiles. Don't go to any town where the Samaritans live. You have plenty to do in reaching just the lost people of the Jewish territories. Tell them that the Kingdom of Heaven is near. Make the sick healthy again and raise the dead. Don't be afraid to touch those with leprosy. Heal them. Drive out the demons. You have received generously; share generously."

"That's quite an assignment, Jesus," one of us commented. "What are we supposed to take with us?"

"You won't need to take any money with you. Travel light. Don't take any extra clothes or other stuff. You'll have no trouble earning your three meals a day."

"That sounds easy enough," another responded. "But I don't understand how we're supposed to get things organized when we get to a town."

"When you enter a town or village, find a good person and stay at his house until you leave for the next town. When you stop at a house, greet them courteously. If they welcome you, respond to their friendliness. Let your peace be with them. However, if they are hostile or unfriendly, leave quietly. It will be hard for them when they die and their souls stand before God."

"How will we find this good person you mentioned?" another asked.

"Men, I want you to understand this is a tough assignment. You will be like a sheep running among wolves. You must be on guard. You'll need to be as smart as snakes. But you must also be as innocent as doves. The Spirit of God will be with you."

"It really sounds like this is going to be a tough job."

"Don't act immature or inexperienced. Some people will be looking for ways to make trouble for you. Because you're my disciples, they'll accuse you and you'll end up in court. Don't be surprised if they even beat on you. You'll be taken in front of governors and kings because of me. When it happens, remember that you have an opportunity to be a witness about me to them and to the Gentiles. Don't worry about what you should say or how to say it. The Spirit of your heavenly Father will give you the words to say."

"You have taught us many things, teacher. We can use the words you have used to teach us."

Jesus warned, "When people realize you are talking about the one true God instead of some feel-good religion, be alert! Family members will turn against each other. Children will even have their parents put to death. Men will hate you because of me. Don't give up. Stand firm with me, and you will be rewarded in the end. You can survive! Before you visit all the cities of Israel, the Son of Man will come."

"Are you telling us that people will actually hate us because of you?"

"You are my students. Don't expect better treatment than the teacher gets. It is satisfactory when the students are like the teacher. You can be sure that if they call me bad names, you will get the same treatment . . . maybe even worse."

"This sounds pretty dangerous."

"Don't be frightened by them. Eventually there will be no secrets. So go ahead and tell them what I have told you. Don't hesitate. Share the good news publicly. Don't be bullied by those who can hurt you physically. They cannot destroy your soul, your spirit. Fear only God for he has your body and soul in his hands."

"It isn't easy to understand how important God really is in all this."

"Ever wonder what you are worth to God?" Jesus asked. "Well, do you have an idea how much a sparrow is worth? If one of them falls to the ground, God knows about it. You're worth more than thousands of sparrows."

"What?" a surprised look passed across the faces of his disciples. "I never thought about being valuable to God," one commented.

"Why, God has even numbered the hairs growing on your head," Jesus said.

"He has?" another responded.

Jesus nodded and went on talking. "Stand up for me to those around you, and I'll stand up for you before my Father in heaven. But if you turn your back on me here on earth, I'll not protect you in front of my Father in heaven. I didn't come to bring peace. I cause trouble."

The disciples looked at each other before one addressed his comment to Jesus. "Well, the religious leaders certainly agree with the fact that you cause trouble. They haven't been pleased at all with what you keep telling the people."

"That's true. People must make a choice about me. Not everyone will choose to follow me. That choice can even cause separation within families. It could result in a man and his father making different choices or a mother and her daughter choosing different options. Sometimes a man's greatest enemies are members of his own family."

The disciples understood. They knew families who disagreed among themselves about what Jesus was teaching.

"Know this for certain," Jesus cautioned. "If you don't love me more than any member of your family, you're not able to be my follower. Take up your cross and prepare for big troubles. Don't even try to look out for yourself. If you do, you can't win. If you're willing to give up your life for me and what I teach, you can't lose."

"That's a wonderful promise, teacher."

"We are in this together," Jesus said. "People who accept you for what you are doing for me also accept me. If they accept me, they accept my Father who sent me. By accepting one of my disciples, a messenger of good news, they are accepting me. If you accept a person who is doing the right things for me, you will get a reward for that."

After a short pause Jesus added, "Just giving a cup of cold water to one of my followers will be rewarded."

Matthew's Story

Chapter 11

Jesus finished telling us what we could expect when we traveled. We said our goodbyes and started on our journeys. After we were gone, Jesus increased his own travel schedule and traveled alone throughout Galilee teaching and preaching in the towns and villages.

Disciples of John the Baptist came looking for Jesus again. One explained, "John is still in prison. King Herod shows no sign of releasing him. John has a question and sent us to find you."

"Well, you've found me. What is the question he wants answered?"

"He wants to know if you are the one the Old Bible prophet said is supposed to come before the Messiah or should we expect someone else besides you?"

"Here is the best way to answer his question. Go back and tell him what you have heard and seen for yourselves."

John's disciples looked at each other and nodded

in agreement. Jesus began a list of all that was taking place. "Tell him the blind receive sight. The crippled walk again. Those with diseases are healed. The dead are raised back to life. The good news is preached to the poor. This will encourage John, I'm certain. Tell him that every man who doesn't lose faith in me will be rewarded."

While Jesus was reminding them of all they had experienced, their facial expressions changed. And when he was done, the entire group gave a spontaneous shout of joy. It's interesting that we sometimes have to be told exactly what has happened. This special time with Jesus encouraged John's followers, and they were ready to return home.

As they were leaving, Jesus turned to the crowd that had gathered. "Many of you went out to the desert area to see John the Baptist. What was it that you really went out there to see?"

There was a variety of responses from the crowd. "Did you expect to see someone dressed in fine clothes?" Jesus asked. "Of course not! People who wear tuxedos and beautiful clothes are not out in the desert. They are in the palaces of kings and presidents."

The idea of John the Baptist in nice clothes made them chuckle. Jesus smiled. "Did you honestly go to see a prophet? Let me tell you something. The man you saw out there . . . John . . . is the one Malachi, the Old Bible prophet, wrote about. He wrote that a man would come to prepare the way for the Messiah. Well, John is that man."

At least some of the religious leaders recognized

the reference to Malachi and nodded.

Jesus continued, "I tell you the truth! No one in human history is greater than John the Baptist. John has been talking about the Kingdom of God. But let me tell you that in God's heavenly Kingdom even the least person is greater than John is now. During the years of the Baptiser's ministry people have been trying to get into God's Kingdom by force. All the prophets and John worked together for one purpose. They worked to prepare the way for the Messiah of God's Kingdom. If you are willing to believe it, John is the ancient prophet who was to come to you."

"Did you hear what I told you?" Jesus asked and waited. "Believe it!"

He saw their confusion and changed the subject. "I've been trying to describe the people of this generation in a way each of you can understand. They are like spoiled children. They want everything their way. They whine, 'We wanted to play and you wouldn't do it. When we wanted to get serious, you weren't interested.'"

"Hey, now. Just a minute..." someone grumbled.

Jesus kept right on talking. "You people criticized John the Baptist because he was so strict and didn't party at all. Now you accuse me of being a drunkard and partying with people who have bad reputations. Your opinions don't really matter at all. I know I'm doing what's right." He paused and looked around.

He thought about all the cities where he had ministered. As he reviewed how his visits were received, he was truly disappointed. In spite of all the miracles he had done, the people did not repent.

Then he named the places where he had been. "Koazin and Bethsaida just wait! You are going to be miserable! If the non-Jewish people of Tyre and Sidon had seen the miracles you have seen, they would have repented a long time ago. Let me tell you, it will be better for those people in Tyre and Sidon on judgment day than it will be for you."

This was a strong charge against them, but Jesus didn't let up. He went right on. "Capernaum, you think you're special. You'll be at the bottom of the list. If the wicked city of Sodom had seen the miracles you've seen, that city would still be standing today. Things will be easier on Sodom on judgment day than it will be for you."

Suddenly, he broke into prayer. "Father, Lord of heaven and earth, I praise you. You have not explained your way of doing things to the people who are proud and conceited. Instead, you chose to show your way to ordinary people. That's the way you do things and I thank you for it."

After the short prayer, Jesus once again turned to talk to the people. His tone was quite different. "I want you to know that my Father in heaven has given me all these things to say and do. This is something He and I are doing together. No one truly knows me except my Father. No one knows the Father like I do unless I choose to let them know Him."

Looking directly into their eyes with compassion

Jesus continued, "Are you tired?" People nodded. "Oh, I'm not talking about physical energy. I'm asking if you are feeling exhausted trying to keep up with all the rules the religious leaders have placed upon you." Their responses left no doubt that they were, indeed, exhausted as they tried to keep the rules.

"Well, I have some really good news for you. You may come and follow me and discover how good life can be. Watch me and I'll teach you how to do what you need to do. I won't put a heavy load of rules on you. You'll learn how to really live."

Chapter 12

After we returned from our teaching journeys, Jesus went for a walk with us. It was Saturday, the Jewish holy day which they call the Sabbath. We were walking through a ripe grain field, and began to pick heads of grain and eat them. The Pharisees who had been following us were, as usual, looking for a reason to criticize Jesus. They called out to him, "Look! Your disciples are breaking the Law again."

"Oh, really? How well do you know your Old Bible history?"

The Pharisees were confident of their knowledge and said so.

"Have you forgotten what David and his men did? When they got hungry, they went into God's house and took the bread that was set apart for the priests. They ate it. That certainly wasn't lawful."

The Pharisees couldn't deny what Jesus said, and he continued. "Surely you have read the Law."

The Pharisees felt put down and had no intention of getting embarrassed the second time. They just stood there and kept quiet.

Jesus asked another question. "Did you forget what happens when the priests do their religious duties in the temple on the Sabbath? That work they do really breaks the rules of the Sabbath. Nevertheless, they are considered innocent."

The religious leaders still had nothing to say.

"You're certainly picky about what is lawful and what isn't!" Jesus said. "Let me tell you, the person who is far more important than the temple and the temple duties is right here with you. Now see if you can figure out what this statement means: 'I desire mercy, not sacrifice.' When you get it figured out, you'll know you should not have condemned the innocent. The Son of Man is greater than the Sabbath."

We didn't hang around in the grain fields to spend more time talking with the Pharisees. We turned and kept right on going to the synagogue in the next town, but those men kept right on following us.

When we reached the next town, we were greeted by a man with a crippled hand. Those religious leaders never gave up. They looked over the situation and figured out what Jesus was likely to do. Then, they tried to trap him with this question, "Is it lawful to heal on the Sabbath?"

"Let me ask you a question. What do you do if you have a sheep that falls into a pit on the Sabbath? Answer me honestly." He waited, but no one spoke.

"Do you leave it there? No way! You rescue it so it will be safe. How would you compare the value of a man with a sheep? Of course a man is worth far more. Let me tell you, it is certainly all right to do good on the Sabbath."

Jesus turned to the man, "Stretch out your hand." The man did as he was told, and his hand was completely restored . . . just as good as the other hand. The Pharisees were furious. They were so angry that they stomped out of the synagogue and began to plot how they could kill Jesus.

He knew what they were planning, so he left that town as soon as the meeting in the synagogue was over. Many people followed him. He healed those who were sick, and he warned them to keep it quiet. Then he reminded them what Isaiah, the ancient prophet, had written:

"'This is my chosen servant. I love him so much and he makes me very happy. I've placed my Spirit upon him. He will declare justice in the whole world. He won't quarrel or yell at you, and he won't be shouting in the street. He's not going to destroy someone who is suffering. He's not going to walk all over people. He will be the one who wins, and his name will bring hope among all those who believe."

He turned to leave. "Don't go yet, Jesus," someone shouted, and Jesus turned in the direction where the voice came from. On the path was a small group of individuals guiding a man who was obviously hurting, so Jesus waited.

Their spokesman said, "Jesus, this man is demon-possessed. He causes trouble for himself and others. He is blind and he can't talk. He really needs you to make him well." The others nodded in agreement. The man stood silent, and Jesus quietly reached out and healed him.

Suddenly, this man who had been blind and also unable to talk could see his friends. He spoke to them, and his speech was easily understood. The people were shocked. In their amazement they asked, "Could Jesus be the Son of David?"

Later that day when the Pharisees heard about this, there was another outburst of anger and frustration. Immediately they declared, "That man, Jesus, is in this with Beelzebub the prince of demons. He's in this with Satan, the devil himself. That's the only way he could possibly be doing this."

The next time Jesus met the Pharisees he reminded them of their earlier comments and said to them, "You Pharisees should understand this simple truth. If a kingdom fights against itself, that kingdom will be ruined. If a family is divided and fights with others in the family, it won't last long. If Satan drives out Satan, he is divided against himself. How can his evil kingdom possibly survive?"

"If I drive out demons by Beelzebub, by what power do your leaders drive them out? If I drive out demons by the Spirit of God, then the Kingdom of God is here. No one can break into a strong man's house and steal his things unless he ties up the strong man first."

"That surely makes sense," a stranger commented.

"Anyone who is not on my side is against me," Jesus declared. "Let me tell you something you really need to understand. Every sin and curse can be forgiven except one. If you curse the Spirit of God, that will not be forgiven. You can speak against me and be forgiven, but if you speak against the Spirit of God that will never be forgiven."

It was obvious the people were listening carefully.

"If you want good fruit, get it from a healthy tree. The fruit from a bad tree is wormy. The fruit lets you know about the condition of the tree".

The Pharisees had heard more than they wanted to hear. A few started wandering away but stopped because Jesus continued talking.

"Your minds are like a snake pit. You say mean and dirty stuff because you have evil thoughts. A good person says and does good things. A bad person says and does bad things because that's what he thinks about. Someday all those careless and hurtful words will come back to haunt you. Words have power. Your words will either help you or make trouble for you"

Later some of the religious teachers and the Pharisees tried to trick him again. "Teacher, we want you to give us a miraculous sign."

"You just want miracles to satisfy your curiosity. Your sign will be a Jonah sign. He spent three days and nights in the belly of a great fish. The Son of Man will be gone three days in a deep grave. That will be your sign.

"You men should learn something from Nineveh.

When judgment finally comes, the people of Nineveh will speak, and they'll condemn you. They repented when they heard Jonah's message. Right now a man far greater than Jonah is here with you, and you quarrel about proof. The Queen of Sheba will also condemn you on the judgment day. She traveled to hear Solomon's wisdom. Yet, someone wiser than Solomon is right here with you, and you argue about proof."

The Pharisees and religious leaders knew he was speaking about himself.

"Let me warn you." Jesus said. "When an evil spirit comes out of a person, it goes looking for a place to rest. I'll explain what happens if it can't find that place.

"It goes back to the place it left and finds the place empty and in excellent condition. The evil spirit invites seven spirits more wicked than itself, and they all move in and live there. Actually the person is worse now than it was at first. That's what you can expect to happen to yourselves." Things were suddenly very quiet.

While Jesus was talking with this large crowd, his mother and brothers showed up outside and let people know they wanted to talk with him. Someone told him who was standing outside wanting to see him.

His response surprised everyone. "Who is my mother? Who are my brothers?" He pointed to his disciples and said, "Here is my family. Whoever does the will of my Father in heaven is my brother and sister and mother."

No one could clearly understand what he meant, but right then was not the time to ask for an explanation.

Chapter 13

Later that same day Jesus went out and sat by the lake. It was not long before a crowd gathered so close to him that he climbed into a boat tied nearby. Jesus often used parables, stories, to teach. That day was no exception.

"Look!" he said, "You people know something about soil so I'm going to tell you a story about a farmer. This farmer went out to sow the seeds. As he scattered the seeds across the field, they landed on four different kinds of dirt.

"Some seeds fell along the side of the road. As the seeds landed on the hard pavement, the birds quickly came and ate them. That's one kind of dirt, the roadside. Some seeds fell on rocky places where there wasn't much soil. At first, the new plants quickly sprang up, but there wasn't enough soil to keep the young roots moist. When the sun came up, the plants were scorched. They withered because their roots dried out. That's the second kind of dirt.

"Other seeds fell among thorns. The thorns and weeds grew side by side. Since the weeds grew faster, they choked the life out of the young plants. That's the third kind of dirt. Fortunately, some seeds fell on good fertile soil and became healthy plants. Some produced a hundred times more than had been planted. Some sixty times and some thirty times more than planted. Good soil is the fourth kind of dirt."

It sounded like he was done. It seemed a long time . . . but it was probably only a few seconds . . . before he said, "If a person has ears to hear, let him hear."

Although many of his listeners worked on the farms, they really needed time to figure out how this applied to them. Even though there was a crowd listening to him, it was the disciples who asked, "Why do you speak to people in these difficult parables?"

I'm sure others wondered the same thing. After all, the special twelve disciples were not the only friends and followers of Jesus who were there that day. Some from the crowd were standing close enough to hear his explanation.

"There are some secrets only disciples . . . true followers . . . can understand," Jesus said. "You disciples have been given the privilege to know the secrets of the Kingdom of Heaven. Those who are not my followers do not have the same privilege. It works like this. "If you pay attention, follow what is being taught, you understand a little. Then you keep learning more and more. But if you don't pay attention or don't like to listen carefully with your heart, you'll soon forget or lose what little bit of understanding you had."

Once more an Old Bible prophecy was fulfilled. Isaiah had written, "You will see, but you won't understand the meaning of what you see. You will hear, but you won't understand what it means. The people quit paying attention. They have become hard of hearing, and they have deliberately closed their eyes. Otherwise they might see with their eyes, hear with their ears, understand with their minds, and turn, and find in me exactly what they need."

To those listening at the water's edge, Jesus said, "Be happy that your eyes are seeing and your ears are hearing. I tell you the truth, many prophets and good men really wanted to see the events you are seeing. They wanted to hear the words you are hearing. But they didn't get the chance."

It took a little time for many of them to get the meaning of what he just said. He waited a short time before asking, "Are you ready to listen some more?" He gave us more time to settle down.

"This is what the parable of the sower and the four kinds of dirt means. It is a story about four different kinds of people and the word . . . the message . . . about the Kingdom of God.

"One man hears the message about the Kingdom of God but doesn't understand it. Then the evil one comes and snatches away the word that was planted in his heart. This is the seed sown along the edge of the road. That's the first kind of person.

"Another hears the word and receives it joyfully at first. This is the seed that fell on rocky places. Soon trouble or persecution comes his way because of the message he received, and since he has no roots and no spiritual depth, he lasts only a short time. Then he quickly changes his mind and turns his back on what he heard. That's the second kind.

"Then there is the man who hears the word, but he is always worrying about everything. This is the seed that fell among the thorns and it is choked out and unfruitful. This man allows his worries and fears for today to crowd out and destroy his faith in God. That's the third kind.

"The seed that fell on good soil is like the man who hears the word and understands it. He produces a crop yielding a hundred, sixty or thirty times what was planted. His faith and love for God grows stronger and stronger. That's the fourth kind of person"

"That explanation helps a whole lot!" the disciples said. You could see the people nodding their heads and smiling to show they understood.

"I have another parable for you. Are you ready to learn some more?"

"Is this one as long and hard as the last one?" a boy in the crowd called out to him.

Jesus smiled but ignored the question. He started the second parable from the back of the boat. "The Kingdom of Heaven is like a man who sowed good wheat seed in his field. One night while everyone was sleeping, his enemy came and sowed weed seeds among the wheat, and then went away. The wheat sprouted and formed heads, and the weeds did, too."

A man in the front row with his feet in the water said something that amused those beside him, but Jesus kept right on teaching. "The owner's servants came to him and said, 'Sir, didn't you sow good seed in your field?'

"'Of course,' he replied emphatically.

"'Then where did all the weeds come from?'

"'An enemy did this,' he replied with a heavy heart.

"The servants asked him, 'Do you want us to go and pull them up?'

"'No,' he answered, 'because while you are pulling out the weeds, you might also pull up the wheat with them. Let them grow together until it's time for the harvest. At that time I'll tell the harvesters to cut and collect all the weeds and tie them in bundles to be burned. Then they will harvest the wheat and bring it into my barn.'"

Jesus offered no explanation to the crowd which was beginning to look puzzled again. Instead, he immediately told two short parables before he ended his teaching for the day.

"The Kingdom of Heaven is like a mustard seed which a man planted in his field. It is amazing that though it is the smallest of all the seeds, when it grows, it becomes the largest garden plant. It becomes like a tree so that the birds come and perch in its branches."

He quickly told another parable: "The Kingdom of Heaven is like yeast that a woman mixed into a large amount of flour until it worked all through the bread dough."

Once again the words of a prophet were fulfilled: "I will open my mouth in parables. I will utter things hidden since the creation of the world."

As Jesus was coming ashore, we could hear the comments from people in the crowd.

"Can something as small as a mustard seed really grow that big? I'd like to see one."

"Well, you should come to my place. I've got a whopper!" a neighbor replied.

"Maybe as little as I have to offer, I can produce some good results," another added.

"I never thought anything I ever had in my kitchen could have something to do with God's Kingdom. I think I'll go take another look. I'll be thinking some more about what he just told us," a housewife said as she hurried away.

Jesus left the crowd and we went into the house where we were staying. After a while, we made this request, "Would you please explain the parable of the weeds in the field."

"The field is the world. The Son of Man is the one who sowed the good seed. The good seed represents the children in the Kingdom of God. The weeds are the children of the evil one. The enemy who sows weeds is the devil, Satan. Harvest time is the end of the world as we know it.

"The Son of Man will send his angels to weed the

garden. They will weed out all those who caused others to sin by doing bad things. The weeds will be thrown into a fiery furnace and destroyed. There will be great sorrow and tears of agony. But the children of the Kingdom will be gathered up and shine like the sun in the Father's Kingdom. If a person has ears, let him hear."

There were the usual expressions of thanks for the additional information. Then Jesus motioned for us to stay. "You need to understand the value of the Kingdom of God. I want to give you two examples.

"The first example is a hidden treasure like a vein of gold. When a person finds the field where the vein of gold is hidden, he sells everything he has. He eagerly buys the field where the he knows the gold is located.

"The second example of its value is like looking for very fine and valuable pearls. When you have finally found the most beautiful pearl, you sell everything you own in order to buy the pearl. You know its value will only increase.

"Because you are all familiar with the lake, I want to share a parable about net fishing The Kingdom of God is like a net that was let down into the lake and caught all kinds of fish. Some of you men were fishermen. Tell me what happens next?"

Peter replied, "Why, you pull it up on shore."

"Then what do you do?"

"You start sorting the catch," John answered. "You keep the good fish and throw those which are not good to eat back into the lake."

"That describes what it will be like at the end of the world as we know it," Jesus said. "The angels will come and separate the wicked from the righteous. The bad will be thrown into the fiery furnace. There will be great sorrow and tears of agony.

"Have you understood all these things?" he asked.

"Yes," one after another replied.

"A religious teacher who knows the Law of the Old Bible and has been taught about the Kingdom of God is like a wise homeowner. He shares both the new treasures as well as those that he has owned for a long time." He let us know he was done teaching for that day.

The next morning Jesus went back to Nazareth, his home town. He began teaching the people in their synagogue, and they were shocked. "Where in the world did this man get all this wisdom? How can he possibly have power to do miracles?" they asked.

"Isn't this the son of Joseph, the carpenter? His mother is Mary and she lives right over there." The lady pointed toward a house close by.

"Aren't his brothers James, Joseph, Simon and Judas? His sisters live here, too, don't they?" The more they talked the more they felt Jesus was a fake, and they rejected him.

But Jesus said to them, "Only in his hometown and in his own house is a prophet without honor."

Jesus didn't do many miracles there because they didn't believe in him. He would be going to other places to do the miracles.

Chapter 14

Herod, the son of the terrible King Herod the Great, was now the king of Galilee and Perea. News about the ministry of Jesus finally reached him, and he was disturbed by those reports. He spoke to the people who worked for him, "This man, Jesus, must be John the Baptist who is risen from the dead! That's the reason miraculous powers are available to him."

The king had a good reason to be upset. On his orders John was arrested about a year earlier, and recently he had him put to death. This happened because of John's preaching. John told King Herod, "It is against the law for you to have Herodias as your wife. She is still the wife of your brother Philip, and you have no right to have her."

Herod was enraged and wanted to kill him, but because he was so popular and the people thought he was a prophet, he was afraid to do it. However, something dreadful happened to change Herod's mind.

During King Herod's birthday celebration, the daughter of Herodias and Philip danced for the guests. Herod was ecstatic with the way she danced for them.

"My dear girl," Herod called to the young dancer. "You danced beautifully. I give you my word that you may have whatever your heart desires equal to half my kingdom." The crowd clapped with pleasure at his generous offer. He was hardly prepared for what happened.

She spoke to her mother. Then she stood before the King and stated her request, "I want the head of John the Baptist on a platter." Herodias smiled a wicked smile when she so clearly heard the bold request. She showed no surprise nor should she. After all, she was the one who told her daughter what to ask for.

Herod felt trapped. He had given his oath in front of his dinner guests, and he could think of no way to save face. So after struggling for a few moments, he ordered that her request be granted. The soldiers went down into the dungeon and cut off John's head. In a few minutes his head was brought in on a platter and given to the young girl. She carried it to her mother who smiled as she took the strange gift.

The next morning John's disciples went to pick up his body and buried it. They went to find Jesus to tell him what King Herod had done.

When Jesus heard the news, we went by boat to a solitary place. Unfortunately, the people heard where we were going, and many from the towns hurried around the lake to meet us. When Jesus came ashore, he saw the large crowd. Although he had wanted to be alone, he had compassion on those who were suffering. He reached out and healed their sick.

It was late afternoon when we went to him and said, "This is an out-of-the-way place, and it's already getting late. We better send the crowd back to their towns and villages so they can buy food."

"Why should they go away? You give them something to eat."

"Have you looked at the size of this crowd? There's no way we can feed them," one of us commented.

"There are hundreds of people here. What can we possibly do?" one asked with an especially strong emphasis on we.

"Yeah, we only have five loaves and two fish."

"Bring them here to me," Jesus said, and we did as he asked. Turning to the crowd, he told them to sit down on the grass and announced, "It's supper time!"

The expression on the faces of many of those in the front said it all. They looked at the size of the crowd and then at the bread and fish. They shook their heads in doubt.

"The size of this crowd is tremendous, and he wants us to have supper?" a doubter spoke up.

"I'm sure we must be covering at least four or five acres. I wonder who is going to serve all of us?" a man asked, and they chuckled together.

"It's hard to believe that we are actually going to

be fed here," a voice in the crowd declared. "But I'm willing to stay and see what happens."

"Don't ever under estimate what Jesus can do," one of us said and gave the man a disgusted look.

Jesus took the loaves and the fish. Looking up to heaven, he gave thanks and tore the bread into pieces. Next he gave the pieces to us, and we passed them to the people. We were busy!

After some time, one of the disciples asked, "Are you sure they really don't want any more?"

"Finally, we're all done. We can't give any more away."

"But you know what's left to do?" a fellow disciple asked. We looked toward the crowd and saw some of the people had baskets. We immediately knew what had to be done.

We picked up all the left-overs which amounted to twelve basketsful. About five thousand men, besides women and children, were fed that day. It was no surprise that we were tired.

"Men," Jesus said to us, "it's time for you to head across the lake. Load up and shove off. I'll take care of the crowd." We moved into action. With our experience on the water, we were soon away from the shore and sailing out on to the lake.

To the crowd Jesus said, "It's been quite a day. May your walk home be quick and safe." With those final words from Jesus, the crowd quickly headed home.

It had been a long day, and it was good to be alone

at last. Jesus climbed up the mountainside away from the stragglers who were still milling around. He longed for time to pray, and the time had finally come.

As the evening settled down around him, he sat there alone in the approaching darkness. His thoughts turned to the tragic death of John the Baptist. And he was very sad.

Meanwhile, the disciples were a considerable distance from the shore and the waves were hitting the boat hard. Sometime between three and six o'clock in the morning, Jesus looked at the storm blowing across the lake. The lightning lit up the sky and there in the distance he could just make out the disciples in the boat struggling against the wind and waves. He knew what he needed to do, so he walked out on the lake toward his disciples.

The first one to see the figure walking on the lake shouted, "Look! It's a ghost." The rest of us turned quickly. We, too, began to yell as fear gripped us.

But Jesus immediately called to us, "Take courage! You don't need to be afraid. It's me, Jesus"

Impetuous Peter shouted, "Lord, if it's you, tell me to come to you on the water."

"Come," he said.

We were all in a state of shock. We watched as Peter . . . always willing to try anything . . . climbed out of the boat.

"Wow, do you see that?" someone asked. "Peter is actually walking on top of the water."

We watched in disbelief. While still looking at

Peter, we heard a huge wave coming toward us. Peter must have heard it too and for a brief moment took his eyes off of Jesus. The sight of the wave scared him, and he began to sink. In panic he yelled, "Lord, save me!"

Jesus reached out his hand immediately and caught him. "You need more faith," he said. "Why did you doubt?"

Jesus and Peter climbed into the boat, and the wind died down. We were convinced and said with conviction, "It is true! You are the Son of God."

Later in the morning we landed at Gennesaret. As soon as the men tending their boats there recognized Jesus, they sent word to all the surrounding area. Almost immediately people began arriving with their sick friends and relatives. They wanted Jesus to heal them.

"Jesus, these people who we dearly love really need your help. We know you are able to heal them. Please come close enough so they can touch your coat," they begged. He did, and everyone who touched him was healed.

Chapter 15

On another day some Pharisees and teachers of the religious law came to see Jesus. They traveled the eighty miles up from Jerusalem to Galilee, and as usual they came with a complaint. "Jesus, your disciples are always causing problems? They don't even wash their hands like they are supposed to before they eat. Why do they break the traditions of our ancestors?"

"And you men think that my disciples are the only ones who ignore traditions? Let me ask you a question. Why do you break God's commandments?" He waited a few seconds before answering his own question. "You break His laws for the sake of your own traditions!"

This is not what those men wanted to hear. They had come to attack, and they were not expecting to be put on the defensive.

"Stop acting so shocked! It looks like I better set the record straight for you."

The Pharisees and teachers enjoyed causing trouble

for Jesus, but they were never ready to be challenged.

"Surely you remember the commandment in the law, 'Honor your father and mother'." Jesus said. "It is followed with this threat 'anyone who curses his father or mother must be killed'. But you know what you and your buddies do? Let me remind you.

"When your parents come asking for help in their old age, you get very pious. You tell them you can't help them because you gave God all of the extra money. That was the money which you should have used to take care of them. So you claim you can't help at all. That is *not* honoring your father or mother.

"You replace God's law with one of your own traditions. You are nothing but a bunch of hypocrites! You are no better than lying thieves!"

The Pharisees were visibly angry. The religious leaders were becoming more hostile each moment, but the onlookers were enjoying every minute of this exchange.

"Isaiah was certainly right when he described religious leaders," Jesus stated. "He told us exactly what to expect. He wrote that you would say all the right things about God, but in your hearts you didn't really plan to do what he asked. Isaiah also wrote that you would act like you were worshiping God but it wouldn't really be worshiping Him. You would teach your own rules about good living instead of His."

There was nothing more for Jesus to say. How could the Pharisees and the religious leaders possibly continue their attack on him now? Jesus just turned his back on all of the men from Jerusalem and walked away.

He walked a few yards, and he relaxed a little bit. Then he spoke to the crowd that had walked along with him. "Listen carefully. I want you to clearly understand what I am about to say." He waited a few seconds before speaking again. Everyone was giving full attention to him.

"You people have a lot of rules given to you about what you can and cannot eat. You've been taught that if you eat certain things it will make you unclean. Let me tell you once and for all. What goes into a man's mouth is not what makes him unacceptable to God. It's what comes out of his mouth when he talks that makes him unclean. Don't ever forget to be on guard about what you say."

A few leaders had stayed around so they could still hear Jesus. After the stern lecture Jesus had given them, they tried to get lost in the crowd. It was quite obvious they were embarrassed and upset. The disciples came to Jesus like tattling school boys, "Do you know the Pharisees were offended when they heard what you just said?"

He replied, "Every plant that my heavenly Father has not planted will be pulled up by the roots. Leave them to their own thoughts. They are blind guides. You know what happens if a blind man leads a blind man. They both will fall into a ditch."

Peter said, "Can you slow down? The blind leading the blind business we can understand. Earlier you mentioned rules about eating and being unclean. We need to have that explained."

"Come on! Don't you get it?" Jesus asked. All of us

were pretty nervous. We looked at Peter and then back to Jesus while we waited to see if there would be an explanation.

"It's really quite simple," Jesus said. "Whatever you eat goes into your mouth, and then travels through your digestive system. The body takes what it needs for nourishment, and then the rest is dumped. That is a simple physical happening." We understood all that. It was the part about what comes out of the mouth that left us confused.

"What you say comes from the heart," Jesus said. That made sense to us, but we wanted more. He continued, "What you say comes from inside you. You are responsible for what you think and say. It is your evil thoughts about murder, adultery, sexual immorality, theft, lies, and slander that make you unacceptable to God. Eating with unwashed hands certainly does not make a person unclean."

We had plenty to think about, but Jesus was ready to take off for another city. He was ready to go some place far away from these religious leaders. Dealing with the Pharisees and those like them took a lot of energy. I'm sure we could even make him tired. Sometimes it seemed we would never understand everything he wanted to teach us. To get away for a while he took us away with him, and we headed for the region of Tyre and Sidon. That was about sixty miles farther north over along the Mediterranean coast in the ancient Kingdom of Phoenicia.

One day on this long walk north, a Canaanite

woman came to him. She was very determined and spoke boldly, "Lord, Son of David, have mercy on me! My daughter is suffering with demon possession, and she really is tormented."

It seemed that Jesus ignored her and did not respond but kept right on walking. Finally, we went to him and urged him, "Please send her away. This is really embarrassing. We can't get her to keep quiet. We don't think she'll ever give up."

"She is not a Jew," he answered. "I was sent only to the lost sheep of Israel."

The woman was stubborn. She followed the disciples to where Jesus was resting. There she knelt in front of him and pleaded, "Lord, help me!"

He replied in a stern manner, "You don't take the children's bread and feed it to their dogs."

"Yes, Lord, I understand what you mean," she said, "but even the dogs are allowed to stay around the table and eat the scraps that fall to the floor."

Then Jesus answered, "Woman, you have great faith! Your request is granted." And at that very moment her daughter was healed.

After some time there, Jesus and all of us left the region of Tyre and Sidon. We walked back the sixty miles from the coast of the Mediterranean Sea to the Sea of Galilee.

When we arrived there, we continued up a mountainside. It was not long before the news was out that we all had returned, and the crowds once again came to see Jesus. There seemed to be no end of those in need. The lame, the blind, the crippled, those unable to speak, and many others were brought to him. And he healed them.

"May the God of Israel be praised!" were the first words uttered by some who were able to speak for the first time. They were suddenly talking in a normal manner and everyone was amazed. A sense of awe swept through the crowd as they listened to the testimonies of those who were healed by Jesus.

"Oh, how beautiful," exclaimed one who was seeing the colorful wildflowers on the mountainside for the first time. "I had no idea what I was missing." You could almost hear the tears in her voice.

"I can walk!" shouted another as he danced around with his friends in praise to the God of Israel.

After three days on the mountainside, in the middle of all the excitement, Jesus called us together. He pointed to the crowd and said, "Look at all these people. I really care about them. They've been with me three days and now they have nothing to eat. I don't want to send them away hungry, or they may collapse on the way."

Always problem-conscious, we murmured among ourselves. It finally dawned on us that Jesus really didn't want to send the people away without feeding them. Fearing his answer, we turned to Jesus and asked in a half-hearted way, "Where could we get enough bread in this remote place to feed such a crowd?"

Jesus always had a solution for every problem. "How many loaves do you have?"

"Seven," one of us answered.

"And a few small fish," another added knowing what was coming next. We walked over to where Jesus was standing and waited. Jesus told the crowd to sit down on the ground. Watching a large crowd find places to sit captured our attention.

When the people were seated, once again Jesus took the loaves and the fish and gave thanks to God for the food. After he had prayed, he took the seven loaves and the fish and gave them to us. We passed the food among the people, and everyone ate until they were satisfied. Nothing was wasted. We picked up seven basketsful of broken pieces that were left over. Four thousand men besides the women and children were fed that day.

After Jesus sent the crowd away and got into the boat, we set sail toward the vicinity of Magadan, a small village south of Capernium.

Chapter 16

We had just reached the edge of the village when someone shouted, "Hey, Jesus." By the tone of voice we knew what was about to happen. Wherever we went the Pharisees and Sadducees always showed up, and here they were again. They approached us.

In a sarcastic manner one of the Pharisees said, "Jesus, we could really understand you and what you are teaching if. . . ."

"Oh, really?" One of us interrupted before the Pharisee could finish. We had enough experience with his kind to make us very suspicious.

Changing to a polite tone he continued. "We would like for you to show us a sign. You know, some sign so we can clearly see and understand what you are teaching." This request was nothing new.

"You want a sign?" Jesus repeated as he looked at the group of men who were there to test him. He spoke directly to them in a stern voice, "You have no trouble understanding the signs in the sky. If the sky is red in the evening, you say 'We'll be having some nice weather.' But in the morning if the sky is red you grumble 'Well, it's going to be stormy today. Just look how red and overcast the sky is.'

"Only people who are wicked and unbelieving want a miraculous sign. Let me make it clear to you. The only sign you will ever have is the sign of Jonah!" With that, Jesus turned and motioned to us, and we all walked away from the trouble-makers. As usual, the Pharisees were unhappy with his response.

Later that day we all headed back across the lake. Although we had spent some time in the village, we forgot to get bread. Before we were very far from the shore, Jesus said "You men need to be careful. You must guard yourselves against the yeast of the Pharisees and Sadducees."

"What is he talking about?" one muttered.

"Pharisees?" another asked.

"Yeast? Oh, my goodness. He's found out we forgot to bring bread," another commented.

"I told you, he'd find out," was a sheepish accusation.

"Come on, you guys," Jesus said as he joined their conversation. "Where is your faith? Do you think I'm upset because you forgot to get bread? Will you ever learn? Remember when you had only five loaves for the five thousand? How much did you gather up afterwards? What about the four thousand? How much that time? I wasn't talking about bread."

"I get it," one spoke quietly as he nudged his companion. "He's talking about the stuff those men have been teaching everybody." Slowly one by one we realized what Jesus meant.

A week or so later he led us to a beautiful forested region in the mountains near Caesarea Phillippi. This is near the source of the Jordan River, and from there it flows about thirty miles south into the Sea of Galilee.

"You men have been spending time traveling around this area. What are people saying about me? Have they told you who they think the Son of Man is?" He was really curious about the people's opinion of who he was.

Though many of us responded immediately, our answers were really quite different.

"Some say John the Baptist."

"Elijah"

"Jeremiah or one of the prophets."

He listened carefully to our answers and then asked a very pointed question. "What about you? Who do you say I am?"

Always quick to respond, Simon Peter answered, "You are the Christ, the Son of the living God."

There was a moment of silence as we looked at Simon and over to Jesus. Jesus replied, "Simon, son of Jonah, you have been blessed, indeed. That is a secret no man could have told you. My Father in heaven let you know that. You are Peter, a rock. On the rock I will build my church. It's going to be so strong that not even the powers of hell will be able to stop it. Access to the Kingdom of Heaven will be available to you. When you say 'no' on earth it will be a 'no' in heaven. A 'yes' in heaven will be a 'yes' on earth. Men, I need your promise. I want you to promise me that you will not tell anyone that I am the Messiah."

Knowing for certain that he really was the Messiah, the Savior of God's people, made us think very carefully. This would be a very serious promise. We were in a very thoughtful mood and grew even quieter as Jesus continued talking.

"I must soon go to Jerusalem," he said. "When I am there many things will happen to me. The elders, the chief priests, and the teachers of the Jewish law will be the ones causing me great trouble. Before they are finished, I will be killed. But on the third day after my death, I will be raised to life." The silence was powerful. We could not believe what we had just heard.

Peter in his usual manner took Jesus away from the group and protested. "There has to be some mistake. Nothing bad is ever going to happen to you. You're the Messiah!"

Jesus turned his back to Peter and began to walk away saying, "Satan, get away from me." Then turning back to Peter he said, "Peter, you don't understand. Your intentions are good, but you are not seeing things the way God sees them. You're talking just like any other man."

We were all discouraged and disappointed now for this was a sad turn of events. Jesus knew how painful this was for us because he could see the pain on our faces.

He spoke softly, "Men, this is the way things are shaping up. If you want to follow me, you have to let me lead. Don't run away from what we're facing. Don't try to save yourself. If you do, you'll be a loser. Instead, let me teach you how to handle things so you'll come out on top. The only way to get what you truly need requires sacrifice. It won't do you any good if you get everything in the whole world but lose yourself. If you follow me, you'll find out what true living means. What price are you willing to pay for your soul?

"This is not the time to allow yourselves to get discouraged. It won't be long. The Son of Man will come with the Father in all his majesty and glory. There will be a band of angels with us. You'll be rewarded for what you've done. You can believe what I am saying. Some of you here are going to see the Son of Man in his Kingdom glory before they die."

What could he possibly mean?

Chapter 17

It was only six days later that three of us saw the glory Jesus had spoken about. He took Peter, James, and John, and they went to the top of a high mountain. There, right in front of their eyes his whole appearance changed. His face was shining like the sun, and his clothes were filled with light. They were whiter than anything they had ever seen. Suddenly, they realized Jesus was not alone. Moses and Elijah, who had been dead for hundreds and hundreds of years, were talking with him.

As this was happening, Peter got up enough courage to interrupt the conversation. "Jesus, it's really awesome that you'd let us be here with you. This is really great! Would it be okay if James and John helped me build three small chapels here . . . one for you, one for Moses, and one for Elijah?"

While he was still talking, a bright cloud came down and covered all of them. From inside the cloud a loud voice announced, "This is my Son whom I love. He pleases me greatly. Listen to him!"

The sound of the voice coming out of the cloud scared them, and they were terrified and fell to the ground. Jesus came and touched them. "Get up," he said softly. "You have no reason to be afraid." When they looked up, Jesus was alone. Moses and Elijah were gone.

As they were coming down the mountain, Jesus instructed them, "You must promise not to tell anyone what you just saw. After the Son of Man has been raised from the dead, you may talk about it as much as you like." The three disciples even promised not to tell the rest of us.

"Jesus," one asked, "why do the religion teachers say that Elijah must come before the Messiah comes?"

"It is true, but Elijah has already come. People didn't know him when they saw him. They treated him terribly. You watch. They're going to treat me just as bad." Then the disciples realized that he was talking about John the Baptist.

A crowd joined us as we sat waiting for them to get down to the bottom of the mountain. As soon as they reached us, a man came and knelt in front of Jesus. "Lord, have mercy on my son," he begged. "His suffering is so horrible he goes out of his mind. Sometimes when the seizures come, he gets thrown into the fire and sometimes into the river. Your disciples couldn't help him at all. They couldn't do anything for him."

"What a generation!" Jesus exclaimed as he looked at us sadly. "Will you ever learn? How long must I stay here with you before you fully understand? Bring the boy to me." Jesus immediately ordered the demon to get out of the boy and it left. He was healed at that very moment.

When the crowd finally left, we went to Jesus and asked, "Why couldn't we drive out the demon?"

"You just don't have enough faith. If you would only have faith the size of a mustard seed, you could tell the mountain to move and it would happen. When you have enough faith, there is no problem you will not be able to handle!"

When we arrived back in Galilee, Jesus told us once more, "The Son of Man is going to be betrayed. Men will kill him, and on the third day he will be raised to life." This really bothered us.

A few days later we all returned to Capernaum. It was tax time. The temple tax collector stopped Peter and asked, "Your teacher does pay the temple tax, doesn't he?

"Yes, he does."

As soon as Peter got back to his house Jesus asked him, "What do you think, Simon?"

"What do you mean?"

"What do you think about taxes?" Jesus asked again. "Who is supposed to pay taxes? Do kings collect taxes from their own sons or from others?"

Peter laughed. "From others, of course,"

"Then are the sons exempt?" Jesus smiled. "Oh, let's not offend them. Let's just pay the tax. Go fishing. There's a surprise waiting for you."

From the look on Jesus' face Peter realized

something unusual was about to happen. He waited for more information.

"It will be the first fish you catch. Open its mouth and you'll find just the amount you need. Take it and give it to that tax collector. It will be enough for my tax and yours."

Chapter 18

During our travels with Jesus, he talked many times about the Kingdom of God. On many occasions we talked about it among the twelve of us. Though we had many discussions, we realized we still had a lot of questions. Finally, one day while we were stopped by the side of the road one asked the question bothering all of us, "Jesus, who is the greatest in the Kingdom of Heaven?" We became quite uncomfortable while we waited for an answer.

He didn't answer immediately. He looked around and saw a child standing nearby with his parents and called to them, "Mother, would you let your child come here for a just a minute or two?" Then to the child he said, "Yes, I'd like you to come here beside me."

The mother and father beamed with pleasure. To have their child chosen by the Teacher was a privilege, indeed. Without delay, the child came and stood beside him.

Then Jesus turned his attention back to us. "You were asking about greatness in God's Kingdom?"

"Yes, we wonder who is the greatest?"

"Well, this may not be the answer you were expecting or hoping for. But I tell you the truth, unless you give up your self-centered ways and become like little children, you won't have a chance to get into the Kingdom of Heaven."

This certainly was a surprise, and we exchanged glances as Jesus continued with his explanation. "The greatest in God's Kingdom are the persons who are truly humble. It's people who are *not* full of a 'look what I've done' or 'just see how much I know' attitude. To be great in God's Kingdom you must be as teachable and ready to learn as this little child."

He ignored what we were saying among ourselves. "I'm not through with this subject yet. You need to understand that when you accept and welcome a child just as I do, you are welcoming me. Hear this! If anyone causes a child who believes in me to do wrong . . . to sin, it would have been better for that person to have a big rock hung around his neck and thrown into the sea to drown."

Jesus sent the child back to his parents while we discussed what he had been explaining to us. The fact that Jesus had not moved away was a good indication to us that he was not finished teaching. In fact he had much more to share.

We sat under a tree as Jesus continued talking. "Do you know why things are so miserable in the world?

114

It's miserable because of all the things that make people sin! Things that cause people to do wrong can be found almost anyplace. But those who create anything that encourages a person to do sinful things is in for *big* trouble!

"In fact, if your hand or your foot causes you to do bad things, get rid of it. It's better for you to be crippled than to have two hands or two feet and be thrown into eternal fire for your sins. And if your eye causes you to do bad things, fix it so you can't see. You would be better off if you were blind than to have two eyes and be burned in the fire of hell."

His words sounded harsh to us, but he wasn't finished. "Don't think for a minute that powerful or wealthy people are more important to my Father than the little children in poor families. Their guardian angels can always contact my Father. Let me tell you a story that will illustrate just how much my Father cares about these children. Then you can tell me what you think."

We always enjoyed hearing his stories. So we got comfortable and ready to listen. Then he told us this story. "If a man owns a hundred sheep and one of them wanders away, what happens?"

"He gets upset."

Ignoring the interruption, Jesus continued, "Won't he leave the ninety-nine safely in the pasture and go to look for the one that wandered off?" We nodded in agreement and Jesus kept talking. "If he finds it, he is one happy man. I tell you the truth, he is happier about that one sheep than he is about the ninety-nine that didn't

115

wander off.

"Now here's the point. Your Father in heaven is not willing that any child should be lost." He waited for us to understand how really important a child was to God.

When someone is teaching, you can never be totally certain why the subject gets changed. But whatever caused it, the topic shifted from a child and the lost sheep.

Suddenly, Jesus started a new lesson. "If someone believes in me like you do but makes trouble for you, go to them . . . and just between the two of you . . . let them know what they did that was wrong. If they listen to you and correct what they did, you've solved the problem and the two of you are still friends."

"What if they won't listen?"

"Well, if they won't listen, take one or two others with you. They can listen as you try once more to solve the problem."

"But sometimes that won't work either, then what are you supposed to do?"

"If they still refuse to listen," Jesus said, "tell it to the church. If they are unwilling to listen to the church, you have done all you can. Their stubbornness and lack of concern for what is right shows that they are no longer believe in me. Treat them as you would a stranger. Continue to pray for them and continue to offer forgiveness. There is a really important lesson here. You must take seriously what you say to one another. What you allow on earth is allowed in heaven, and what you forbid on earth is forbidden in heaven.

"Let me be emphatic. If two of you agree when you ask my Father, it will be done for you by my Father in heaven. And if two or three of you meet together in my name, you can be certain that I am there with you." Jesus concluded the discussion.

Though the group broke up to stretch, Peter still had some concerns about this entire area of conflict between fellow believers. It wasn't long before he walked over to talk to Jesus.

"I heard what you had to say about settling problems, but I have a question. How many times, Lord, must I forgive the guy who keeps doing the same wrong thing to me? Is seven times enough?"

"Peter, I tell you, you must never set a limit on forgiveness. Let me tell you a story about forgiveness." Peter always seemed to learn easier when Jesus told a story, so he listened carefully.

"A king was ready to settle the accounts with his officers. He was surprised to discover that one of them owed him ten thousand pounds (4,554 kilos) of silver. He called that officer to discuss payment. Since he was unable to pay the debt, the king ordered the man, his wife, his children, and all his possessions to be sold to slave traders to pay the debt.

"The officer fell at the king's feet and begged for mercy. He promised he would pay back everything. The king felt sorry for him, and he canceled the entire debt and let the man go free.

"However, when this officer left, he went to find

another of the king's soldiers who owed him forty-two and a half pounds (19 kilos) of silver. He grabbed him by the throat and started yelling, 'Pay me what you owe me!'

"This second man fell on his knees and begged for time. He, too, promised to pay back everything he owed. But the king's officer wouldn't listen. He had the man put in prison until his family could pay the debt.

"The other officers of the king found out what had happened. They were upset and reported the whole story to the king.

"Then the king called for the first officer. 'You are a wicked man,' he said, 'I canceled all of your debt because you begged me to. Why didn't you have mercy on your fellow soldier just as I had on you?'

"The king was angry. He turned his officer over to the jailers to be punished. Now he had to pay back all ten thousand pounds of silver he owed the king."

Jesus looked directly at Peter and said, "You can expect the same kind of treatment from my heavenly Father unless you forgive your brother from your heart."

Nothing more needed to be said. Peter had plenty to think about.

Chapter 19

When Jesus knew his time in Galilee was finished, he led us south into Judea and then across the Jordan River. We could escape neither the crowds nor the physical needs they brought to him. While there, he kept on healing those who came to him in faith.

This trip to Judea was no different from our earlier travels. We were almost certain to find three things: crowds, physical needs, and religious leaders. This time was no exception. Some Pharisees were ready with another question in their endless effort to trap Jesus. They asked, "Do our laws permit a man to get a divorce for whatever reason he might have?"

"You profess to know Jewish history and the Law, so I am sure you have read what the law permits. A man will leave his parents' home and unite with his wife and they become one. You know that! If they are one in the sight of God, no man should try to pull them apart."

"If that is true," they asked, "why did our great

Jewish leader, Moses, say a man could get rid of his wife? He said to give her a letter of divorce and it would all be over."

"That was not God's way then, and it is not His way now. Moses gave you permission to divorce because your hearts were sinful and you thought only of yourselves. Here is the real truth. If a man divorces his wife and marries another woman, he commits adultery. The only exception is when a wife breaks her marriage vows to her husband and is no longer faithful to him."

Then one of us said, "If that's true, a man is stuck. It might be better to never get married."

"Marriage is not for everyone. Some never give it a thought. Others never get a chance to get married. Some stay single to focus on the Kingdom of Heaven. Those who can accept the responsibilities of marriage should go ahead and get married."

The exchange between the Pharisees and Jesus was interrupted by parents who were crowding in with their children. They wanted him to put his hand on each one and pray for them.

"Can't you see that Jesus is busy," we said to the parents. "You shouldn't be bothering him to pray simple blessings over your kids."

"Just a minute, fellows," Jesus said. "Don't blame their parents for bringing them. Let the children come. The Kingdom of Heaven belongs to people like them." He took time to pray for them. When he had prayed for the last child, he said goodbye to the children and began to walk further down the road.

We had only walked a short distance when we heard a man calling, "Teacher." Jesus waited for him. "Teacher, what good thing must I do to have eternal life?"

"That's an important question. Why ask me about what is good? Only God is good. Obey His commandments."

"Which ones?"

Jesus began naming them. "Don't murder, don't commit adultery, don't steal, don't lie to anyone, honor your father and mother, and love your neighbor as much as you love yourself."

"That's fine. I've kept all those. Is there something else I still need to do or is that it?

"If you want to do your very best, go, sell everything you own and give the money to the poor. Then your treasure will be in heaven. After you have done that, come and follow me. Become one of my disciples."

The young man's expression changed. His shoulders drooped, and he slowly walked away. He wanted to keep his wealth, and he had a lot of it.

As the young man walked away sadly, Jesus said to us, "This is the truth. A rich man finds it very hard to enter the Kingdom of Heaven because of his love for his wealth. By comparison, it is easier for a camel to go through the eye of a needle than for a rich man to get into the Kingdom of God."

We were shocked! We asked, "Who can get into God's Kingdom if the rich can't?"

Looking at us, Jesus said, "No man can possibly

enter God's Kingdom on his own. He must have God's help. If God is involved, nothing is impossible."

Peter questioned, "O.K. Then what will happen to us? We left everything to follow you!"

Jesus smiled and said, "Let me assure you about your future. In the new creation when the Son of Man sits on his majestic throne, there will be a special place for you. You that followed me will help me rule. The twelve tribes of Israel will be judged, but it won't just be you twelve doing the judging. Everyone who has left all they have to follow me will receive a hundred times more than they gave up. More important than that is the gift of eternal life for each one."

We took it all in and were pondering the future when he added, "There will be some surprises. Some of those considered important will be at the end of the line. Some considered insignificant will move to the best places."

We were stunned! We sat waiting for Jesus to explain.

Chapter 20

In just a few minutes Jesus continued the discussion.

"I want to tell you another story. The Kingdom of Heaven is like the owner of a large farm who was looking for hired hands. Early in the morning he went to the employment office to hire some men to work in his vineyard. It was urgent to get helpers at once. The grapes were ready to be picked. He agreed to pay each man the normal full day wages, and his offer was accepted. He sent them into his vineyard.

"About nine o'clock that same morning he needed more workers. So he went back to the employment office looking to hire some more. There were some men still standing around, and he offered to pay them whatever was right. They accepted his offer, and he sent them to the vineyard immediately.

"As the day went on, he discovered that he still needed more men. At noon and again at three o'clock in the afternoon he hired more men. Finally, at five o'clock he was desperate. The job had to be finished today and the present crew couldn't get it done. He went once more to the employment office. He was pleasantly surprised and relieved to find some men who were not working. The landowner asked them, 'Why have you been standing here all day doing nothing?'

"'Because no one hired us.'"

"'Well, I need you badly. If you want to work, you should go to my vineyard,'" and he hired them to work the rest of the day.

"At the end of the workday, the owner of the vineyard told his foreman to call the workers. "Pay them what they've earned. You should begin with the last ones hired.'

"Those who were hired at about five o'clock came to the foreman. Each man received a full day's wage. He paid the same to each group. Since they had worked all day, those who were hired first came to the foreman expecting to receive more. But each one of them also received the same pay. They looked at their pay and they were angry. They went looking for the landowner to complain.

"'"What do you mean by this? These guys who were hired last only worked one hour. 'They're getting the same pay we got. We did most of the work. We were working out there in the vineyard during the hottest time of the day!.'

"Men, I am not being unfair to you," the landowner

told them. "I have paid you exactly what we agreed on. It's my money. I can do whatever I want to with it. Are you trying to tell me that I don't have the right to do what I want to with my own money? Or are you envious because I am generous? Now, take your pay and go.'

"So the last will be first, and the first will be last."

We were all stumped. We couldn't say the owner didn't have the right to control his own money, but it still didn't seem fair. No one said a word, and Jesus left us to solve our problem without his help.

On the way up the mountain to Jerusalem, Jesus wanted us to get away from the crowd so he took us over by the side of the road. "We are going up to Jerusalem and you must be prepared for what will be happening. There the Son of Man will be betrayed to the chief priests and the teachers of the law. Listen carefully to what comes next. First, they will condemn the Son of Man to death. Then, he will be turned over to the Romans. Finally, he will be mocked, beaten, and crucified. On the third day he will be raised to life!"

No one had anything to say. We just stood there and endured an awkward silence.

Before we continued on the way to Jerusalem there was one more interruption. The wife of Zebedee and the mother of his sons, James and John, was traveling with the group. She knelt in front of Jesus and waited for permission to speak.

"What is it you want?"

"I have a special request to be filled when you are

established in your Kingdom. Please let one of my sons sit at your right and the other at your left."

"You have no idea what you are asking," he said to her. Then he said to James and John, "Can you drink the cup I am going to drink?"

"We can," they answered.

He said to them, "Yes, in the years to come you will, indeed, drink from my cup."

Turning back to their mother he said, "I have no authority in the seating arrangements. That's my Father's decision. He alone knows for whom they have been prepared."

This whole episode upset the rest of us. It really wasn't their fault, but we were very angry with the two brothers because of their mother's request. Jesus stepped in to cool things down. "Let me explain something. You all know the Roman rulers really enjoy lording it over people. Their top officials enjoy pushing us around. That's not the way God does it. Whoever wants to be top leader among you has to be the servant. Whoever wants to be first must follow my example. The Son of Man did not come to be served, but to serve. He came to give his life to pay the ransom for many."

By this time, as we left Jericho and began the steep climb up the mountain, the crowd around Jesus had become huge. We hadn't gotten too far from Jericho when two blind men sitting by the roadside heard that Jesus was walking by. They shouted, "Lord, Son of David, have mercy on us!"

The crowd told them to be quiet. The blind men were determined and shouted all the louder, "Lord, Son of David, have mercy on us!"

He stopped near them. "What do you want me to do for you?"

"Lord, we want our sight."

Because of his great compassion, Jesus touched their eyes. Immediately they received their sight and could see clearly. They didn't ask where Jesus was headed, but they followed him anyway.

Chapter 21

As we were approaching Jerusalem, we came close to Bethphage. Jesus spoke to two of us. "I want you to go over into the village."

"Is there a problem, teacher?"

Without responding to their question, Jesus gave these instructions. "As soon as you get into the village, you will find a donkey tied there with her colt beside her. Untie them both and bring them to me"

"What happens if the people try to stop us?"

"If someone says anything to you, just tell him that the Lord needs them," Jesus said, "and he will send them with you right away."

As they headed for the village, they had no idea that they were helping to fulfill the words of the prophet, Zechariah.

'"Tell the Daughter of Zion here comes your king. He is gentle and comes riding on a donkey, on a colt, the foal of a donkey."

Planning to take something that didn't belong to them was a new experience for the two disciples, but they had learned to trust Jesus. They had no problem finding the donkey and the colt.

"I've never seen you men before," a by-stander shouted as they were untying the donkey. "What are you doing there?"

"The Lord needs them," they quickly answered, but they sounded a little uncertain. To their amazement, the man just nodded and let them go. Jesus must have arranged this in advance they thought.

They eventually caught up with the rest of us, and they were leading a donkey and a colt. It was obvious that something special had been developing while they were gone. The crowd was getting larger and the excitement increasing. People cut branches from the palm trees and laid them on the road. Others put their coats on the animals. Some even placed their coats on the road that led to Jerusalem. Then, Jesus sat on the donkey and it walked forward.

It was shaping up like a parade. As we traveled the last few miles to Jerusalem, some people went ahead of Jesus. Others joined us as we went along. We followed him as he rode among the crowd. People were shouting:

"Hosanna to the Son of David"

"Blessed is he who comes in the name of the Lord!"

"Hosanna in the highest!"

As we entered the gates to the city, it soon became obvious that the citizens of Jerusalem were not expecting a celebration. They certainly were not anticipating a parade coming into town. People came from all sections of the city asking, "What's going on? Who is that man on the donkey?"

"Don't you know? Weren't you expecting him? This is Jesus. He's the prophet from Nazareth in Galilee. Surely you know about the miracles he has done!"

The parade moved through the city and finally stopped at the entrance to the temple. Jesus dismounted and went straight into the court yard. This open area was filled with merchants selling those things needed for the Jewish Feast of the Passover. The tables of money changers were everywhere since the people could not use Roman money to buy the sacrifice to be offered on the altar.

What happened next was a shock to everyone. Jesus began knocking over the tables and benches of the money-changers and the merchants. He forcefully drove them from the temple. He was shouting, "My house will be called a house of prayer. You merchants know the words from the prophets. Look what you have done to it! You have made it a den of robbers. You've been cheating people so you could make large profits."

Even though the action of Jesus scared many, the blind and the lame were not afraid to approach him there in the temple. He healed them right there even though the chief priests and the teachers of the law saw what he was doing. They also heard the children shouting in the temple, "Praises to the Son of David." They were irritated.

"Do you hear what these children are saying?"

"Yes, I hear them. Haven't you read that part in the Old Bible where God said that He even intended for infants and children to give praise?" With that Jesus left them in the temple and we walked the five miles to Bethany where we spent the night with some friends.

Early the next morning as we were returning to Jerusalem, Jesus saw a fig tree. He was hungry and went to the tree to get some fruit, but he found it had nothing except leaves. While we were all looking at it, he said, "You will never bear fruit again!" The tree withered immediately.

"How did the tree dry up so quickly?"

Jesus replied, "You don't yet understand what you can do if you have faith. If you believe . . . without doubting, you can do more than what was done to the fig tree. You can say to this mountain, 'Move over into the sea,' and it will be done. If you believe, you will receive whatever you ask for when you pray." We were still amazed and confused.

By the time he finished this lesson, we had reached the temple, and once again entered the temple courtyard. While he was teaching, the chief priests and the elders came. "By what authority are you doing these things? Who gave you this authority?"

"Before I answer, I have one question for you. If you answer me, I will tell you the source of my authority for doing these things." They voiced no objection and Jesus asked, "John's baptism . . . where did it come from? Was it from heaven, or from men?"

They discussed it among themselves. "He's tricked us again. If we say from heaven, he will want to know why we didn't believe him. But if we say from men, the people will be after us because they believe John was a prophet. Boy, are we stuck!"

Frustrated they answered, "We don't know." The religious leaders were becoming angry, but they stayed around to listen to what Jesus had to say.

"Fine, then I won't tell you by what authority I am doing these things.

"Let me share a story with you, and then you can tell me what you think.

"There was a man who had two sons. He said to the older one, 'Son, I want you to go work in the vineyard today.'

"'Well, I'm not going out there in the hot sun, Dad.'

"The work needed to be done. It couldn't wait, so the father went to his other son and gave him the same order. This son immediately answered, 'Sure, Dad, you can count on me.' But he didn't go.

"In the meantime, the first son thought it over, changed his mind, and went out into the vineyard and spent the day woking.

"Which of the two sons honored his father's request?"

"The first, of course," they answered.

"Understand this truth clearly," Jesus told them. "The tax collectors and the prostitutes are entering the Kingdom of God ahead of you. John the Baptist came to show you the way of righteousness. Oh, you went out to hear him all right, but you didn't believe him. The tax collectors and the prostitutes did. Even when you saw this happening, you still didn't repent and believe him."

The silence was deafening. The religious leaders just stared at him with red faces.

"I have another parable for you. A landowner planted a vineyard and put a wall around it. He dug a special place where they could press the grapes into wine, and he also built a watchtower. He rented the vineyard out to some farmers and left on a long journey which he had been planning for some time.

"When it was time to pick the grapes, he sent his servants to check things out. They went to collect the landowner's share of the fruit.

"But this is what happened. The farmers grabbed his servants. They beat one, killed another, and stoned a third. When he learned what had happened, the landowner sent more servants than he had the first time. The farmers treated them the same way as they did the first group. Finally, he sent his son to them. 'They will surely respect my son,' he said.

"He was terribly mistaken. When the farmers saw that it was the landowner's son who came to collect the rent, they began plotting. 'This is the young heir. If we kill him, there's no one left to get his inheritance. We'll own it all.' So they captured him and threw him out of the vineyard and killed him.

"What do you think the landowner will do with

those farmers when he comes back?"

"That's easy to decide," someone answered. "Those farmers were criminals and deserve drastic punishment."

"The landowner will certainly find other farmers who will share honestly," another declared.

After a moment Jesus said, "Surely you have read in the Old Bible that 'God's capstone is the stone that was rejected. This is what the Lord has done. We think it is marvelous!'

"I am telling you the facts." Jesus concluded the discussion with the Jewish leaders when he said, "The Kingdom of God will be taken from you. It will be given to those who will produce fruit. If you fall on the stone, you will be broken into pieces, and if the stone falls on you, you will be crushed."

The chief priests and the Pharisees thought about the parables they had just heard. Suddenly, they realized he was talking about them. They were angry and wanted to arrest him right then. But they were afraid of the people around them who thought Jesus was a prophet.

They decided to wait for another time.

Chapter 22

Jesus continued speaking to the crowd in parables even though he knew the Pharisees in his audience were angry and frustrated.

"Listen to this story. The Kingdom of Heaven is like this king who had prepared a wedding banquet for his son. He called his servants and told them, 'It's time now. You know the people to whom you took the invitations earlier. Go tell everyone who was invited that the banquet is ready.'

"The servants followed instructions and scattered throughout the countryside looking for those who had been invited. As they saw each invited guest, they announced, 'The banquet for the king's son is ready. It's time to come.'

"One after another the guests declared they were not coming. The king's servants pleaded, 'You're supposed to be leaders of the kingdom and friends of the king. You've had plenty of time to take care of everything and be ready for his son's wedding banquet.'"

The words of the servants had no effect, and they

returned to the palace without any guests.

"When the king learned no one came, he sent out a second group of servants. His instructions were more urgent. 'Tell them the wedding banquet is all ready. The meat is cooked and everything is ready for them at my son's wedding dinner. Tell them to come now before the food is spoiled.' The servants left to bring the invited guests.

"Once again the servants visited each of the invited guests with the king's urgent message. 'The king sent us once more to remind you that it's time to come to the wedding banquet. Everything is ready.'

"One landowner stated, 'Well, you can tell the king I can't come. I have to go check on some of my property.'

"At the home of another invited guest they were told, 'I won't be there. I have to take care of some of my business affairs.'

"Some of the invited guests even grabbed the king's servants. 'You evidently didn't hear us when you were here the last time,' they said. They became very rude and kicked the king's servants out of their homes. Some servants were even killed.

"When the king heard what had happened, he was enraged. He gave this order to his officers, 'Send the army and destroy the murderers and their cities.' The orders were carried out.

"The king walked through the huge banquet room and looked over all the food that was ready for the feast. He had prepared a magnificent wedding feast, but the
138

invited guests all refused to come. His heart was heavy.

"He called more of his servants and said to them. 'Here's the plan. You know the circumstances. We're not going to be defeated. I want you to go out into the streets of the city, and when you find someone there, give them an invitation to come and enjoy the wedding banquet for my son.'

"There was a sense of urgency when this group of servants left. Whenever they saw someone they called to them, 'Hey there, I've got some good news for you. The king has prepared a wedding feast for his son. It's all ready. You're invited to the feast at the king's palace. Go right now!'

"One after another the foreigners, the beggars, and the poor whom they found on the streets accepted the invitation. Finally, they had found enough people to fill the giant banquet hall, and they returned to the palace.

"The king came into the room to greet his guests. Suddenly, he noticed one man who stood out in this crowd of strangers. He walked over to him, looked closely, and then inquired, 'How did you get in here? You don't have on the wedding clothes. You aren't dressed to celebrate with us. You don't belong here.' The man was speechless.

"The king told his attendants, 'Take that man. Handcuff him. Bind his feet. Throw him outside. He belongs in the darkness. There will be weeping and painful agony. Many are invited, but few are ready to come.'"

After that, the Pharisees began making even more plans to trap Jesus by using his own words. They returned a few hours later with some of Herod's officers. "Teacher," they said, "we all know that you are honest and teach God's truth. We know you aren't persuaded by what people think about you. So we want your opinion about taxes. Is it right to pay taxes to Caesar?"

"You cheating phonies! Why do you keep trying to trap me? Show me a coin you use to pay your taxes." They handed him a coin. "Take a good look at it. Whose picture is there?"

"Caesar's," they replied.

"Here's an easy answer to your question. Give Caesar what is his, and be sure to give God what is God's."

It wasn't long before the Sadducees, another group of religious leaders, came to see Jesus. They don't believe there is any resurrection. Nevertheless, they came with a trick question. It clearly was going to be a full day of testing for Jesus.

"Teacher, Moses told us what we were supposed to do if a man dies without having children. His brother was supposed to marry the widow and have children for him. Now, this man had seven brothers."

Jesus knew what they were planning, but he listened courteously anyway.

The Sadducees continued. "The first brother married and died and since he had no children he left his wife to one of his brothers. The same thing happened again clear down to the seventh brother. Finally, the woman died without having any children. Please tell us, at the resurrection, when we join God in heaven after we die,

140

whose wife will she be? After all, she had been married to all seven men."

"Well, it's obvious you haven't read your Old Bible carefully, and you don't know the power of God. At the resurrection we'll be like the angels in heaven. We'll be beyond marriage. Now, let's clear up something about the resurrection of the dead. You must understand that God is the God of the living. Read again what was written.

"It was written 'I am' . . . not was . . . 'the God of Abraham, the God of Isaac, and the God of Jacob.' He is not the God of the dead but of the living."

The crowds were again astonished at his teaching.

When the Pharisees heard that Jesus had gotten the best of the Sadducees, they were ready again to try to embarrass him. They chose one of their smartest men who supposedly was an expert in the law. This was his test question: "Teacher, according to the Jewish law which is the greatest commandment?"

"The most important commandment is to love the Lord your God with everything you've got . . . your heart or your emotions, your spirit, and your intelligence. The second requires you to love your neighbor just like you love yourself. Everything in the Law and the prophets in the Old Bible hangs on those two pegs."

While they were all trying to trap him, Jesus turned the table and put them on the spot. "What do you think of Christ, the Messiah? Whose son is he?"

He caught them off guard, and they quickly replied, "The son of David, our greatest king in our history."

"I have another question then. If Christ is the son of David, why did David call him Lord? Remember, David was guided by the Spirit of God. Here's what David said, 'The Lord said to my Lord: Sit at my right hand until I put your enemies under your footstool.'

"If David calls him 'Lord' how can he be his son?"

The Pharisees were stumped. To avoid further embarrassment they quit asking him questions and did their best to get lost in the crowd.

Chapter 23

Whenever Jesus met with the Pharisees, you could usually count on one thing. You'll learn something. Today was a good example. "There is something you must not forget," Jesus told us and the crowd. "You are to obey the Pharisees and the teachers of the law."

"Why should we obey them, Jesus? They're always trying to trap you. That's certainly not good," one of us declared.

"You're right about the trap," Jesus answered. "That's not good. However, they are the ones who inherited the authority of Moses. That's the reason you must do what they tell you. You can trust what they teach about Moses. Obey that part. But don't do like they do. They don't do what they tell you to do."

"Was Moses the one who gave us all these rules?" someone inquired.

"Moses gave some rules, but you have to watch out and be on guard to know which ones," Jesus replied. "The religious leaders like to load you down with their rules, and some are rules that Moses didn't teach. Trying to keep all their rules becomes a heavy load to carry. They don't do a thing to make it easier."

"There are surely a lot of rules to follow," someone whispered.

"They like to be the center of attention," Jesus said. His voice sounded like he was really disappointed in the way the Pharisees behaved. He continued, "I'm sure you have noticed their prayer boxes. Even if the boxes or lockets are small, you can't miss them when they are strapped on their foreheads. But these religious leaders make theirs bigger than most, so you can't fail to see them. You cannot fail to notice the long prayer tassels on their garments either."

Smiles were visible throughout the crowd. Though people tried to muffle the snickers, they could still be heard. People understood exactly what Jesus was describing.

"Another thing you will notice," he continued, "is their desire to have the most important seats wherever they are, whether at a banquet or at the synagogue. Of course, they expect to be recognized publicly. They also expect you to address them as a Religious Teacher.

"Stay alert! Keep your relationships clearly in mind. There is only one Master; you are all equals. There is only one Father, and he is in heaven. There is only one Teacher, the Christ. If you try to puff yourself up, you'll get the wind knocked out of you. The truly great people are those who serve willingly." The crowd waited. It was clear that Jesus had more to say.

Needless to say, the religious leaders were not happy with the way Jesus was picturing them. The worst was not over for them yet. Jesus turned in the direction where many of them were standing and spoke directly to them.

"You there . . . teachers of the law and Pharisees . . . are in big trouble! You are big phonies! You refuse to enter God's Kingdom, and you make it difficult for anyone else to get in.

"You're in big trouble, for you are blind guides! You should listen to yourselves. You say it doesn't mean a thing if you swear by the temple. Then you claim that if you swear by the gold of the temple, it's serious and you're bound by your promise. That doesn't make any sense at all. It's the temple that makes the gold sacred. The gold doesn't make the temple sacred.

"Do you ever pay any attention to what you say? You say that if you swear by the altar, it doesn't mean any thing. However, if you swear by the sacrificial gift that's on the altar, it's serious and you're bound by your promise. You are blinded by your own stupidity! The altar is what makes the gift sacred.

"Let me make it clear once and for all. Anyone who swears by the temple swears by it and by the God who dwells in it. Anyone who swears by heaven is swearing by God's throne and by God who sits on it.

"You phonies! You are in big trouble! You give

careful attention to the small stuff. But you forget about the parts of the law that really matter . . . justice, mercy, and lasting commitment! There's nothing wrong with taking care of the little things, but don't neglect the really big issues while you do that. That's like straining on a gnat in your throat and swallowing a camel.

"You religious leaders are such phonies! You're in big trouble! You are so careful to make yourselves look good, but that doesn't change what you really are. If you would just clean up the inside first, the outside would take care of itself.

"You're in big trouble! You phonies! You're like a cemetery with manicured lawns and polished grave stones, but six feet down you have nothing but decay and dead bones. You may impress people by acting like saints, but you know it's really only an act.

"You're in big trouble! You phonies! You build monuments to the prophets and take care of the old burial grounds. You brag about how much holier you would have been than anyone else if you had lived back then. You claim you never would have been a part of those who killed the prophets. You're so foolish. You're criticizing your own ancestors. You're no different than they were!

"You're a nest of poisonous snakes! How do you think you will avoid being condemned to hell? Prophets and teachers are being sent to you even today. You will kill, and yes, you will crucify some of them. Some of them will be beaten in your synagogues. Others will be driven from town to town. You're headed for big trouble! The blood from the murder of good people . . . from Abel to Zechariah, son of Berekiah whom you murdered in front of the temple . . . will be on your head. All of this will be upon you before you die."

Everyone was in shock. Nothing could be said. There was no defense the religious leaders and Pharisees could offer. Jesus turned and looked tenderly through the temple gate toward the city of Jerusalem.

Then he said at the top of his lungs, "O Jerusalem! You will kill those that are sent to you. You have no idea how often I wanted to reach out to protect you. I wanted to protect you like a hen protects her chicks under her wings. But you didn't want me. Take a look how depressing it is. One final word and I'm leaving. You will not see me again until you say, 'Here he comes. He is blessed by God and comes to rule.'"

What did all this mean? Everyone was stumped.

Chapter 24

After his exchange with the Pharisees and the other religious leaders, Jesus left the temple. He and the disciples walked toward Mount Olive just outside the city wall. One of the disciples stopped to look back at the temple which stood on the highest hill in the city. The rest of us stopped, too.

"Jesus, look at that temple!" the disciple requested. "The buildings are so beautiful! It really is a wonderful place for worship."

Jesus turned and looked toward the temple. "Do you see all these things? Take a good look. What you see will all be destroyed. Every building there will become nothing but ruins." We had no idea what he was talking about. It had taken hundreds of years to build the temple and all the buildings around it. We could not imagine how it would ever be totally destroyed.

When we got to Mount Olive, Jesus called us aside and sat down with us. We were alone. "You've been telling us about a lot of things," one of us said to him. "When is all this going to happen? How will we know it's the end of the world as we know it? What sign will tell us you are coming?"

"Let me remind you that first of all you must always be alert. You will hear many men claiming, to be the Christ, and many will believe them. Don't be one of those who is deceived! Don't be alarmed by all the wars between nations. Don't get upset over the rumors about war. Those things will happen, but it's not the end. Some places may have earthquakes for the first time. Weather conditions may not be normal. This can cause crop failures which may result in mass starvation. That's just the beginning."

Sounding a bit frightened, we asked, "What's going to happen to us and all your other followers?"

"It won't be easy. You will be mistreated. Some will even be killed. You'll be hated by people all around the world because of me. It will be a sad thing, and many will quit believing in me. They will hate one another and hand over each other to the authorities who will be against me. Some preachers will show up and claim to be prophets although they are not. A lot of people will be fooled."

"That sounds pretty bad."

"Actually it sounds really awful!"

Jesus agreed. "It will be more evil than it has ever been before. People will not love and care for others like they used to."

"This sounds so frightening and depressing. Is there any good news?"

"Yes, there is some good news," Jesus said. "Those who continue to trust in me to the very end will be saved. But that's not all!"

"What else? We can stand more good news!" More of us were beginning to share the questions.

"Well, the gospel will be preached in the whole world. There will be people in every nation who believe in me. They will witness and teach about me wherever they live. The end will come after that has been done."

He continued, "I want to be certain that you understand. Daniel, the prophet, described what it would be like. The temple and the things used for worship will be abused and will not be treated with respect any more. This will cause misery. When that happens, those living in Judea should flee to the mountains.

"No one should take anything from their home, and those working outside should not go home to get anything. It will be a difficult time for pregnant women and nursing mothers. You should pray that you won't have to escape on the Sabbath or any other time when public transportation is limited or in the winter."

We looked at one another with growing concern. You could almost feel the fear we were experiencing.

Jesus looked around the group and continued. "It will be the greatest destruction since the world began. It will never happen like this again. It will be so bad, that if God didn't set a time limit on the destruction, no one would survive. He will shorten the time for the sake of those he loves. False preachers will appear. They will do great miracles to deceive any believers they can. Now, I have warned you ahead of time."

No one looked relieved. We were all waiting anxiously for Jesus to continue . . . hopefully with some good news.

"When someone tries to tell you that the Son of Man is here or he's there, don't believe it! You'll know when the Son of Man comes just like you know when lightning crosses the sky. In those terrible days people will crowd together like vultures which circle over dead and decaying animals."

We could stand the suspense no longer. A nervous voice whispered, "What is going to happen then?"

"Unusual things will take place. The sun will be dark. The moon won't give its light. Stars will fall from the sky, and the heavenly bodies will tremble."

We were gripped by the frightening predictions of things to come, and our comments revealed the depth of our fears.

"Then the Son of Man will appear in the sky. All over the world those who are not ready will panic. The Son of Man will come in on the clouds. It will be spectacular! His power and glory will be seen by everyone. The trumpets played by his angels will sound more fantastic than you can imagine. From all parts of the world the chosen ones, chosen because they love God, will come to be with him."

With that announcement, it was time to let out a sigh of relief, and we broke into a celebration. We just found out that the good guys win in the end! The saved ones will be safe with Jesus.

"You can learn something from the fig tree. You know its twigs get tender and it starts budding in summer. Well, when you see these things happening that I've been describing to you, it will almost be time for the Son of Man to appear. This is the truth. This world will continue until all these things have happened. Everything ever known in heaven and earth will disappear, but what I say about the Kingdom of God will never pass away."

Jesus paused.

"Tell us when this will take place." we begged, but we were half afraid to find out.

"I can't do that. The angels in heaven don't even know when it will happen. The Son of Man doesn't know the day or hour either. Only the Father knows when it will take place."

We looked at one another in amazement. Surprise was written on our faces. We thought that Jesus knew everything. At least he always seemed to have the answers.

"I can tell you this," Jesus spoke softly. "It's going to be just like it was in the time of Noah. The people just kept doing all the normal things. They ate, slept, celebrated weddings, and did all the usual things. They didn't have a clue about what was going to happen until Noah entered the ark and it began to rain. The endless raining and flooding took them all by surprise.

"That's how it will be when the Son of Man comes.

Two men will be on the job, and the one who is ready for me will be taken. Two women working together will experience the same thing. The one that is ready will be taken.

"Be ready! You have no idea when your Lord may show up. You need to understand this. If the homeowner knew a burglar was coming, he would be there to protect his property. Count on it. You must stay ready because you don't know when the Son of Man is coming."

"That certainly makes sense," we said to one another. "We can do that for sure!"

"Picture this. A man puts a trusted employee in charge of his home while he is gone on a long trip. He doesn't tell him the exact time when he will be coming home. The employee is instructed to feed everyone when it's time."

"He better do that, too," Peter shouted. We all chuckled.

"You're absolutely right," Jesus added smiling. "It will be good for him if he is following his orders when the man gets home. You can believe me. His next job will be better because he was faithful and did exactly what he was supposed to do.

"Suppose, however, that the employee has other ideas besides working so hard. He says to himself, 'Hey, my boss is certainly staying away a long time. I'm going to have a little fun while he's gone.'

"So he begins to mistreat the people who work under him and spends time just goofing off. Suddenly, one day the boss shows up when he wasn't expected. You can count on it. That lazy and unfaithful employee will be punished. He'll lose his job, and he won't have money to pay his rent or buy food. He will be with the phonies where there will be great pain and suffering."

Chapter 25

Jesus wanted us disciples to understand all we could about the Kingdom of Heaven. One day he told us this story. "The Kingdom of Heaven will be like ten bridesmaids who were getting ready for the wedding day.

"As they worked and waited, they divided into two groups. There were five in each group. One group was always working hard to get things ready for the wedding. The other group took things much more casually.

"One day one of the bridesmaids in this busy group announced to her four friends, 'We need to do some more shopping.' The other four agreed. These bridesmaids were the type who always planned ahead.

"'Why in the world would you want to spend time shopping?' asked a member of the other group.

"'Well, we want to be certain we have enough oil to light the lamps we'll carry at the wedding,' the leader explained. 'We don't know for certain when the bridegroom will arrive and the celebration will begin. We want an extra supply of oil just in case he comes later than expected.'

"The bridesmaids who were not a part of the planning group laughed among themselves. 'Oh, we'll have plenty,' one of them said. 'Don't worry about us. Our lamps will be burning brightly when the bridegroom arrives.'

"The planners bought the extra oil and arrived at the site of the wedding and the banquet. They poured the extra oil into containers and kept them nearby. They tried always to be ready. When it was time for the wedding, all ten bridesmaids lit their lamps and went to the front door to wait for the bridegroom to arrive. Those who had extra oil took it with them. As it turned out, the bridegroom was delayed, and all the bridesmaids became sleepy. One by one they fell asleep with their lamps burning.

"Finally, at midnight they heard the announcement, 'Get ready. The bridegroom is on his way! Come out to meet him!'

"The bridesmaids were excited when they were awakened by the news. Each one lifted her lamp to welcome the bridegroom. Suddenly, there was the sound of alarm among those who did not have an extra supply of oil. 'Help, our lamps are going out!'

"They went to those who had purchased extra oil. 'Give us some of your oil!' they begged.

"'We can't do that. We may not have enough for both you and us. You'll have to hurry and go to the store to buy some for yourselves.'

"While the five foolish bridesmaids were trying to

find someplace to buy oil at midnight, the bridegroom arrived for the wedding. The five bridesmaids who planned ahead were ready. They went in with the bridegroom to enjoy the wedding and the banquet.

"Some time later the guests in the banquet room heard a pounding at the front gate. It had been locked because it was so late at night. Then, they heard some loud voices. 'Sir! Sir! Open the door. We're bridesmaids, too.'

"The bridegroom replied, 'The bridesmaids are here. I don't know who you are.'"

Then Jesus warned his listeners, "Keep watch. You don't know when the Son of Man is coming. You must always be ready."

We could tell Jesus wasn't finished. We stirred a little and waited for him to begin again.

"The Kingdom of Heaven is like a businessman going on a trip. This businessman always planned ahead.

"He called his managers together and told them, 'I'm planning to be gone for a while. Unfortunately, I'm not sure how long I'll be gone. Each of you will take care of a part of my business and some of my investments while I'm gone. I'll be giving instructions to each of you before I leave.' He had everything planned. He knew his managers well and planned to give duties to each manager according to his proven ability to manage and take care of things.

"To the first manager he said, 'You've been with me for years. While I'm gone, in addition to your other duties I want you to take care of these investments worth twenty-five pounds (11 kilos) of gold.'

"To the next he said, 'You've been with me for a few years. While I'm away, please take care of these investments worth ten pounds (4.5 kilos) of gold.'

"To the last one he said, 'You have worked for me a short time. While I'm gone, I want you to take care of these investments for me. They are worth five pounds (2.2 kilos) of gold.'

"After giving his instructions, he told each man goodbye and left on his trip.

"The man with the investments worth twenty-five pounds of gold managed the money wisely. In fact, he doubled his money. The man with investments worth ten pounds of gold doubled his money, too. The man with investments worth five pounds of gold didn't use good judgment. He locked the gold away to keep it safe.

"Eventually the businessman returned. One by one he met with his managers to get the report on his business.

"To the first he said, 'Tell me what you did with the investments I left with you?'

"'Sir, you gave me investments worth twenty-five pounds of gold. I am ready to give you investments worth fifty pounds of gold. I doubled your money.'

"'You did a great job!' the business man exclaimed with enthusiasm. 'Your good work will be rewarded. I'll put you in charge of many more departments. Let's go out to dinner together.'

"The next day the man with the investments worth ten pounds of gold reported to his boss. 'You made me responsible for investments worth ten pounds of gold while you were gone. With some hard work, I was able to double it. I now have investments worth twenty pounds of gold to give back to you.'

"The businessman expressed approval of his work and said, 'Good job! I'm going to place you in charge of more departments. Let's go have lunch.'

"When the man with investments worth five pounds of gold showed up that afternoon, the boss could tell he was very nervous. He couldn't look his boss in the eye. He kicked at the floor. Finally, he made his report very fast. 'Sir, everyone here knows you are a hard man to satisfy. You make money off of investments you didn't make. You profit from the work of others. I was afraid of what you might do if I failed, so I decided the safest thing to do was hide your investments in a safe place. That's what I did. Here are your investments just as you left them with me.'

"'You are one lazy undependable employee. You knew I made money on investments I didn't make. You knew that I collected profits from other people's work. You didn't even try! Why didn't you think to put the money in the bank? Then I would have at least earned some interest.'

"The businessman called to another of his managers and gave these instructions. 'Take the investments worth five pounds of gold from this man, and give it to the one who grew my investments to fifty pounds. Tell this to all of my employees. Everyone who has made money for me will get more to work with and each will earn plenty for himself. The person who has not made very much money for me will lose his job. Throw that worthless manager into the street where there will be no jobs for him. He will have much misery for years to come.'"

Once again we were a little nervous when Jesus leaned forward and said, "When the Son of Man comes, it will be in great glory and splendor. All the angels will come with him. He will sit on his throne as king and all the nations will come to him. He'll separate the people into two groups just like a shepherd. The sheep will be sent to his right side. The goats will go to his left."

"Do you mean he's going to separate the good people from the bad people?" one of us asked.

"That's right. Those on the right are the people who have been blessed by my Father. They are to claim their inheritance. They'll be invited to enter into the kingdom God has prepared for them. It's been prepared since the world was created."

The oh's and ah's were easily heard.

"The good man is invited to be on the right side because when I was hungry, he gave me something to eat. When I was thirsty, he made sure that I had something to drink. I had no place to stay, and even though I was a stranger he invited me to stay with him. If I needed clothes, he got them for me. He looked after me when I was sick, and he came to visit me when I was in prison."

"Then the good man will say, 'I don't know when this happened. I never saw you hungry and fed you. I never saw you thirsty and got you a drink. Stranger? When did we ever invite you in and get clothes for you? We never saw you sick or visited you in prison. I don't understand.'"

Jesus smiled as he told us, "I'll let you in on the secret. Whatever you did to help my brothers . . . even those who didn't seem important . . . it was as if you did it for me."

"What about those on the left side, Jesus?" someone asked. "What about them?"

"That's the sad part. I will tell them to leave me for they are cursed. They'll be in the eternal fire that was prepared for the devil and his angels. Here are the reasons they will be forced to depart. I was hungry and they gave me nothing to eat. I was thirsty and they gave me nothing to drink. I had no place to stay and they left me without housing. I needed clothes and they ignored my need. I was sick and in prison, and I never heard a word from them.

"Oh, they will have a lot of excuses and claim they were being accused of things that never happened. It will be of no use. I will tell them that because they paid no attention to those who didn't seem important, they paid no attention to me.

"The bad, wicked people will be sent away to everlasting punishment. Those who served me by serving those in need will have eternal life."

We had much to talk about on the way to the home where we were staying.

Chapter 26

Soon the greatest Jewish holiday of the year was to be celebrated. "Men, you know that Passover is only two days away. The Son of Man will then be handed over to be crucified." Jesus made the statement in a very matter-of-fact way.

Meanwhile, in Jerusalem, the chief priests and the elders were meeting at the palace of Caiaphas, the high priest. No one there was identified by name.

"Well," an elder spoke, "what are we going to do? This man, Jesus, is a constant embarrassment to us."

"That's certainly true," another added. "He makes us look bad. Besides that, his followers seem to keep growing in numbers. The city seems to be full of them."

One more chimed in, "It doesn't make much difference what we say. He turns it around in front of everyone, and we end up looking dumb."

"There's only one solution," the first man said. "We have to get rid of him as soon as possible. The only way that will happen is to kill him."

"You think that will be easy as popular as he is?" another asked.

"Easy? Of course not! But it has to be done . . . and soon!" a man shouted.

"Whatever you do," Caiaphas said, "must not be done during the Feast of the Passover."

One of the chief priests who had been listening carefully cleared his throat. "That's for sure. It needs to be done while everyone is in their homes and with their families. If we tried to do it when his followers are around, we could easily have a riot. This must be done in a very sly manner, so *we* don't get blamed."

They talked some more, and when they finally agreed on what they needed to do, everyone left the palace. The members of this plotting group went their separate ways.

When Jesus was planning this trip to Jerusalem, he accepted the invitation of Simon the Leper to stay in his home in Bethany. One evening a group of men were sitting around the table there at Simon's house when a woman burst into the room. "What's she doing here?" whispered one of the disciples.

No one answered, but all eyes followed her as she walked across the room and stood behind Jesus. No one spoke. They were in a state of shock. This stranger, this woman, broke open a very valuable jar of extremely expensive perfume. The aroma spread through the room like a fresh breeze.

Finally, overcoming our shock, one of us shouted, "Hey, what do you think you're doing?" Before anyone could stop her, she poured the contents of the alabaster jar on Jesus' head.

"What a waste!" one of us said angrily.

"Just look at what you've done!"

"That could have been sold for a lot of money, and that money could have been used to help the poor," another added.

"Why are you bothering her?" Jesus asked sadly as he looked at us. "What she has just done is beautiful! Pouring the perfume on my body was done to prepare me for burial. You better believe this. Whenever the gospel is preached, she will be remembered. By the way, there will always be poor people wherever you go, but you won't always have me with you."

Sometime after this extravagant display, Judas Iscariot, one of the twelve disciples, went to the chief priests. "I know you guys want to get rid of Jesus. How much will you pay me if I hand him over to you?"

The men he was talking to were the religious leaders and supposed to be good men. They were good in name only as they welcomed a traitor into their presence. The men looked from one to another with a wicked gleam in their eyes. What they said was not recorded. Perhaps it was such an evil thing they were doing that no one wanted to keep a record of it.

One of the priests went to the safe and got the money bag containing silver. He opened it and started counting out the coins. One . . . two . . . three . . . four . . . five . . . six . . . seven . . . eight . . . nine . . . ten . . . The count went on. No words were spoken. The clinking sound continued as one coin after another fell in a pile on the table. Judas watched the pile grow. Twenty-five . . . twenty-six . . . twenty-seven . . . twenty-eight . . . twenty-nine . . . thirty! The sound stopped. No one said a word.

Judas scooped up his money, dumped it into a bag, and slinked away into the night. From that moment on, he waited for the best chance to deliver Jesus to the chief priests.

Eventually, it was the first day of the Festival of Unleavened Bread. "It's time to start getting ready for the Passover meal, Jesus," John said. "Where do you want us to go to fix the dinner?"

"I'll tell you where to find a certain man in the city. When you find him, tell him the teacher said it's almost time. Tell him that I'm going to celebrate the Passover with my disciples at his house." They did as they were told, and they made sure the meal was prepared.

When Passover evening came, all twelve of us disciples were at the man's house sitting around the table with Jesus. While we were eating, Jesus, very quietly, gave us some shocking news. "I'm telling you the truth. One of you will betray me into the hands of those who want to kill me."

Speechless would hardly describe our reaction. Slowly we grasped the meaning of his words. One after another we began to ask, "Surely not I, Lord?"

"It's not me, Lord, is it?"

"The one who just dipped his bread in the sauce with me is the one who will betray me. This is just like it was written about him. He's in very big trouble. It would have been better for him if he had never been born."

Then Judas, the one who had taken the money to hand over Jesus, said, "It's not me. Is it teacher?"

"Yes, Judas. You know you are the one."

In silence we continued eating. Soon Jesus took the bread, prayed over it, and tearing it apart he gave it to us. Then he said, "Eat this bread. This is my body." Then he took the cup, blessed it, and offered it to us. He said, "Drink it, all of you. This is my blood of the new covenant. This is done in order for sins to be forgiven."

He paused, then broke the silence saying, "I want you to know that this is the last time I'll drink of this fruit until we drink it together in my Father's Kingdom."

After supper was over, we sang a hymn and then left the house. We started walking toward Mount Olive, a place we often went with Jesus. On the way he told us, "The Old Bible writer knew about tonight. He wrote that the shepherd would be struck and all the sheep would run away. It will happen just like he said. But after I have risen, I'll go ahead of you back up to Galilee.

Peter spoke up, "I don't understand exactly what you mean, but I'm certainly not going to run away."

"Peter," Jesus answered kindly, "just wait and see. Before the rooster crows, three times you will deny that you even know me."

"That's not fair. Even if it costs me my life, I'll never deny you!"

We all said the same thing.

When we got to Mount Olive, we went to the garden called Gethsemane. "Men," Jesus said, "sit here while I go on a little farther to pray."

He asked James and John, the two sons of Zebedee, and Peter to go with him. As they walked a little further in the garden away from the rest of us, his expression changed. He became very sad and obviously bothered. He said to the three with him, "I am so overwhelmed with sorrow I could almost die. I want you men, my close friends, to stay here and watch with me."

By now it was late in the evening. He left them sitting on the lawn and went a little further down the path. He was so loaded with sorrow that he fell face down to the ground. "Father, please can you take this terrible thing from me? Is it possible?"

The agony was intense. For a brief time it seemed like there was an unspoken conversation between Jesus and his Father. The silence was broken when Jesus said, "No, don't do what I want. I want to do whatever you want."

After talking with God a while longer, he walked back to the three disciples. They had fallen asleep. That was easy to do after eating a big meal and walking in the late evening air, then sitting quietly in the garden. Shaking them, Jesus said, "Couldn't you even stay awake and watch with me for just one hour?"

To Peter he said, "You have such a willing spirit,

but you are so human and weak. Be on guard and pray that you don't fall into temptation and sleep again."

Once more he left his three friends and went to pray, "My Father, if you cannot take this terrible thing from me, I will do what you want done."

Coming back later, he found his disciples sleeping again. This time he did not disturb them. He went back to the same spot and prayed the same prayer for the third time.

They were still asleep when he returned. This time he spoke, "Are you still sleeping? Look, my time is up. The Son of Man is about to be betrayed into the hands of sinful men. You better get up now. Here comes the one who is going to betray me!"

While he was talking, Judas, one of the chosen twelve, arrived in the garden. There was a large crowd following him, and they had swords and clubs with them. The crowd was sent by the elders and the chief priests.

Judas, the betrayer, had given the crowd a signal. He had told them, "The one I kiss is the man you want. Arrest him."

After Judas entered the garden, he went immediately to Jesus and said, "Greetings, my teacher!" Then he kissed him.

"Friend, do what you came to do," Jesus replied.

As Judas stepped back, men stepped out from the crowd and grabbed Jesus and placed him under arrest. When that happened, one of Jesus' friends reached for a guard's sword. He drew it and struck one of the servants of the high priest. The blow was strong enough to cut off the man's ear.

Jesus ordered his disciple to put the sword away where it belonged. "If you live by the sword, you'll die by the sword. Don't you realize I could call on my Father, and he would make twelve legions of angels available to me? But things won't happen that way. If it did, what is written in the Old Bible could not be happening now."

He turned to the crowd. "What are you doing with swords and clubs? You don't need those to capture me. I sat in the temple courts teaching day after day, but you didn't bother to arrest me then. But I understand why. You are doing exactly what the prophets said you would do."

Seeing Jesus surrender so quickly frightened us, and we turned and ran to get away at once.

The men who arrested Jesus took him directly to the high priest, Caiaphas. The religious teachers and the elders were waiting there for him. Peter, who had sounded so brave earlier, followed . . . but not too closely. He followed to the courtyard of the high priest's palace and sat with the guards to learn what was going to happen next.

The chief priests and the Sanhedrin, which was the Jewish high court, were eager to get their hands on Jesus. They were not interested in the truth. They wanted to put him to death and were looking for any evidence to help them do that legally. In spite of the number who came before the court and lied about Jesus, they couldn't find

172

any evidence that people would believe

Finally, two men testified, "This fellow," pointing at Jesus, "said he was able to destroy the temple of God and rebuild it in three days."

The high priest arose and said to Jesus, "Are you going to answer? Is their testimony true?" Jesus didn't speak.

The silence annoyed Caiaphas, and he said to Jesus, "I order you under oath to tell us. Are you the Christ, the Son of God?"

Raising his head, Jesus looked straight at Caiaphas before replying, "Yes, just as you said. But I want to tell you that in the future you will see the Son of Man sitting beside the Mighty One and coming from heaven."

Caiaphas was furious with this answer. He ripped his clothes and shouted, "He has spoken against God. That is blasphemy! Why do we need any more witnesses? You heard him. What do you think?"

"He deserves to die!" the members of the Jewish high court answered . . . almost in unison.

After their decision, many walked up to Jesus and spit in his face. On orders, the guards beat him. Some hit him from behind and others mocked him by saying, "Prophesy to us, Jesus. Tell us who just hit you from behind."

Out in the courtyard it was a different scene. A servant girl came and stood where Peter was sitting against the wall. As she looked down at him, she said, "You were with Jesus of Galilee!"

"I don't know what you're talking about," Peter denied in front of everyone.

Peter decided it was time to get a little farther away from the pesky girl. He went out by the gate to the palace courtyard. Another girl saw him standing there and shouted to the people, "Hey, here's one of them. This fellow was with Jesus of Nazareth!"

This time Peter denied it with an oath, "I don't know that man!"

Before long others from the crowd went to Peter and said, "Surely you are one of them. You're from up in Galilee. Your accent gives you away."

Peter let loose a string of curses and swore to them, "I tell you. I don't know the man."

The crowd was silenced by Peter's violent outburst. Everyone clearly heard the rooster crow. Then Peter remembered the words of Jesus, "Before the rooster crows, you will deny me three times."

Turning, he ran from the crowd. He went out and cried in agony because of what he had just done.

Chapter 27

Many talks and debates were held throughout that night. Finally, in the early morning, a decision was reached. The chief priests and elders concluded that in order to make it legal, Jesus must be put to death by the Roman government. So they bound him and took him to Pilate, the imperial governor from Rome.

Judas who betrayed Jesus was there throughout the night listening to everything. When the verdict was given, he was overcome with regret. He hunted for the chief priests with whom he had bargained to deliver Jesus. Finally, when he found them he said, "Men, I've made a horrible mistake. I have sinned."

"Get out of our way, Judas," the Jewish religious leaders said as they pushed him aside so they could get ready to go to the governor's palace.

"You don't understand," Judas cried out to them as they started to walk out of the room. "I have betrayed an innocent man!"

"So what?" they mocked Judas. "That's not our problem."

"But don't you realize this is blood money you gave me?" he shouted.

"That's your responsibility. It has nothing to do with us," they answered as they disappeared through the doorway.

All hope for changing anything that had happened that night was gone. Judas ran to the temple where he threw the thirty pieces of silver on the floor. He kept on running until he got beyond the city wall. Crying with deep regret, he suddenly stopped. Before long the tears stopped flowing down his cheeks. He had killed himself.

Meanwhile, in the city the chief priests gave no sign of disappointment. They were not upset by Judas' words. They picked up the silver coins. "That man is hopeless," one said.

They laughed sarcastically.

"He was happy to get the money earlier. I guess he just can't make up his mind," a second said jokingly.

A third priest added, "We do have a problem. This really is blood money. We can't put it back in our regular funds."

"True," answered the first. "We'll have to use the money some other way."

After talking it over they decided to use it to buy a plot of land outside the city called the potter's field. They would use it as a burial ground for foreigners. To this day it is still called the Field of Blood.

176

More than six hundred years earlier Jeremiah, the prophet, had foretold this event with all its details. He told the exact amount Judas would be paid, thirty pieces of silver. He even wrote that the religious leaders would use the money to buy the potter's field outside the city of Jerusalem.

As the morning sun began to rise, Jesus had already been taken to stand before Pilate, the governor. The governor asked him, "Are you really the king of the Jews?"

"Yes. It is true just as you said."

After that statement, the chief priest and the elders had many more questions for him. They accused him of many things. Jesus just stood there with his head bowed, silent, and exceptionally calm. Finally, Pilate turned to Jesus, "Don't you have anything to say for yourself? Didn't you hear all these accusations?" But Jesus didn't say even one word in his own defense. Pilate was shocked that he didn't want to try to clear his name.

Pilate was a Roman politician who needed to keep things in the city under control. He saw where this trial with its phoney charges was headed. It was obvious to him that Jesus had been brought to him only because the religious leaders were extremely jealous of his popularity.

At the time of this annual Passover Feast, Pilate dared not forget his established tradition. He made a mental note of those who were held in prison awaiting execution. Which of them would be an acceptable "gift of freedom" to offer these worrisome Jews?

The least likely of prisoners the people would want

177

released would be Barabbas. Other prisoners were just as guilty as he was, but everyone, it seemed, knew Barabbas. He was well-known and hated.

Pilate looked at the crowd gathered below his balcony and raised his arms for their attention. When the crowd was silent he shouted, "People, you know it is my custom to release a prisoner each year during your Feast. Tell me, which prisoner would you like released?"

While he was addressing the people, he got a note from his wife. She had written, "I just woke up from a bad dream which really upset me. Jesus was in my dream! That man is innocent. Don't get mixed up in this situation." As he read her note, Pilate knew he was trapped. The people were his only hope for justice.

What he didn't know was that the chief priests and religious leaders had been moving around in the crowd. They were stirring up the people against Jesus and they were urging the crowd to ask that Barabbas be released.

"People! Give me your answer. Which prisoner do you want me to release to you? Jesus or Barabbas?"

"Barabbas," they shouted.

Learning this, Pilate was disappointed but not really surprised. He raised his hands and waited for silence.

"What do you want me to do with Jesus who is called Christ?" Pilate asked even though he was afraid what their answer might be.

They answered as one voice, "Crucify him!"

"Why? With what crime is he to be charged?"

They screamed even louder, "Crucify him!"

This was not the reaction that Pilate had hoped for. The crowd could soon turn into a mob unless something was done quickly. He spoke to one of his butlers, "Bring me a bowl of water."

It seemed a strange request, but no one questions the Roman governor. The bowl of water was placed on the table in front of Pilate. Slowly he placed his hands into the water and took a bar of soap and began washing his hands. Shaking the water from his fingers he declared, "I am innocent. This man's blood is on your shoulders. This action is your responsibility!"

The crowd answered him, "We don't care. Let his blood be upon us and on our children!"

When he heard their response, he told his guards to let Barabbas go.

The crowd waited until the guard returned with the prisoner. What a sight! They welcomed a known criminal. An innocent man was to be prepared for death. Pilate turned to his officer, and, as was the custom with prisoners, he ordered Jesus to be whipped and handed over to the soldiers to be crucified.

The governor's soldiers took him into the Praetorium, the palace barracks. It was their job to carry out Pilate's orders and prepare Jesus to be killed. They called the entire company of soldiers to come see their new prisoner. They knew who he was for Jesus was well known in the whole country.

A husky soldier yelled in a threatening tone, "Strip

him down. Those filthy clothes aren't fit for a king."

"Here's what he needs," another soldier shouted as he threw an old suit of clothes to a buddy close to Jesus.

"Great fit!" The crowd of soldiers laughed as Jesus was forced to put on the formal clothes that seemed so strange to him.

While all this was happening, some of the men had been collecting thorny branches out in the yard. As they twisted the branches together their fingers were pricked, and they jumped in pain. They finished a crown of thorns as quickly as they could. All eyes were fixed on the officer as he carried the rough crown to where Jesus was standing. Then he deliberately shoved it down on the head of Jesus as blood spurted out.

"We need one more thing," a soldier declared in hushed tones. Some turned their eyes from the bleeding head of Christ to follow the spokesman as he walked toward Jesus. He brought a staff and placed it in the right hand of Jesus. It was a cheap substitute, but it was almost like one a king would hold while sitting on his throne. Then this soldier knelt down in front of Jesus like a man would before a powerful king.

The jeers of the soldiers were mixed with the mocking shouts, "Hail, O king of the Jews!"

Several stepped forward and laughed as they bowed before him. Some spit on him. Another soldier took the staff from Jesus and used it to hit him. Then it was passed to his friend who did the same thing, and then he passed it to another. Finally, when they grew tired of this cruel game, they had Jesus put his own clothes back on. It was now time to lead him out to be executed.

As they left the barracks and started down the main street, they met a foreigner standing in the roadway. His name was Simon, and he was a big man from Cyrene, a city in North Africa. They grabbed him before he knew what was happening. They forced him to carry the heavy wooden cross on which they would crucify Jesus.

After walking all through the city, they reached Golgotha. This was a hill outside of the city walls. It was the place the Romans commonly used for executing criminals. Before the final part of this whole ordeal was to begin, they offered Jesus something to drink, but he refused it. They stripped his clothes off of him again and demanded that he lay down on the wooden cross. Then, they used large spikes to nail his hands and his feet tightly to the cross.

This was nothing new to them. They casually lifted the cross and its suffering occupant, moved it over the hole which had been dug to hold it, and let it drop in place. Jesus now hung on a cross that stood between the two criminals, crucified earlier, one on each side. In their calloused manner the soldiers gambled while he hung above them dying. They even rolled dice to see who would get the clothes they had stripped from him.

As the people were watching Jesus on the cross, the silence was broken. "Oops, we've forgotten a very important honor for this king!" a soldier joked.

"Oh? What's that?"

"Get a marker and some wood. We must let everyone walking by here know who he is." They got the necessary materials. When they were finished, they nailed a large sign above his head. It read, THIS IS JESUS, THE KING OF THE JEWS. There he was, an innocent man, crucified with a criminal on his right hand and a criminal on his left.

People came out of the city to stare at Jesus. Others came to make fun of him and shouted, "Hello, Jesus, how's the work on the temple going? You said you could build it in three days. Can you save yourself?"

"Come on down from your cross if you are the Son of God," someone yelled from the back of the crowd.

The chief priests, the teachers of the Law, and the elders joined in this disrespectful joking and laughing. "Look at this man who saved others," they said, "but now he can't even save himself."

"Behold the King of Israel!" some mocked. "Come down from your cross now and we will believe you."

"Oh, yes, he's the one who said to trust God," a teacher spoke. "Let his God rescue him now." Even the robbers crucified on each side of him heaped insults on Jesus.

At noon the mood of the crowd changed drastically. They began to feel unsure and sensed a disturbing presence of evil. Darkness began to settle over the whole area. At three o'clock that afternoon in the eerie quiet of the crowd, Jesus looked up to the black sky and spoke very distinctly, "Eloi, Eloi, lama sabachthani?" which means, "My God, my God, why have you turned your back on me?"

Some of the watchers thought he was calling out to the ancient prophet Elijah. A nervous soldier ran and got a sponge which he filled with vinegar. He put it on a pole and offered it to Jesus. "Hey there, man. I got you something to drink."

"Haven't you done enough? Don't bother him," an on-looker shouted.

"We'll see if your prophet Elijah can help," the soldier replied.

Jesus cried out loudly once again. He released his spirit in death. At that very moment, across the valley in the temple a huge curtain dividing the tall building into two sections was torn into two pieces. It was torn from top to bottom. No man could have done that. Then, there was an earth quake. Tombs broke open and people who had died walked out of them alive. During the following week many of these people went into Jerusalem where they were seen by many.

The Roman officer in charge of the execution of Jesus felt the sudden earthquake. He and those with him saw the strange things that were happening, and they were terrified. "This man really was the Son of God!" he declared. He was truly confused as he tried to understand what was happening.

Many women who were followers of Jesus had come from Galilee for the Passover Feast. They were there, heartbroken, and watching, but not too close. It was this faithful group of women who were always ready to help:

Mary Magdalene, Mary the mother of James and Joses, and Zebedee's wife.

Later that afternoon, Joseph, a rich man from Arimathea, went to Pilate. He had become a disciple of Jesus though not many seemed to know it. "Pilate, your honor," Joseph spoke. "I would like to have the body of Jesus for burial."

This was a brave request because it was contrary to the Roman custom. Usually the victims were just left hanging there on the cross. In view of this, it was surprising that Pilate granted the request.

Immediately, Joseph hired workers who took the body of Jesus down from the cross. Then he made burial preparation and placed the body of Jesus in his new tomb which had just been cut out of a rocky hillside. When the burial of Jesus was finished, he had a stone rolled in front of the tomb to close the entry to the tomb. It seems that when he left he didn't see Mary Magdalene and the other Mary nearby who had been there watching everything that had been done.

By this time, the chief priests and the Pharisees were getting a little nervous. They talked among themselves and finally decided to go see Pilate. The next day, after the Preparation Day Feast, they had an appointment with the governor.

"Your honor," they said, "this has been a troubling time and we hesitate to say anything. However, we remember that when Jesus was alive, that deceiver had the nerve to say he would rise again after being dead three days. We believe it would be in your best interest to place a guard at his tomb. If you don't, his disciples could easily come and steal his body. Then they could tell everyone that he had risen from the dead. Believe us. That would be bad news for you and for us."

Pilate was easily convinced. He turned to his officer and ordered, "Take a guard and make sure the tomb is kept secure." They followed orders and it was done. The tomb was secured by the placing of Pilate's seal on the door and the posting of the guards outside.

Chapter 28

When the Sabbath was over, at the dawning of the first day of the week Mary Magdalene and the other Mary went to visit the tomb of Jesus.

Before they got to the tomb there was another earthquake. One of God's angels came from heaven and rolled the stone away from the doorway of the tomb, and then he sat down on the stone. His clothes were pure white and his appearance was as sharp as lightning. The guards were terrified and seemed unable to move.

As the women approached the tomb, the angel spoke in a most gentle voice, "You have no reason to be afraid. Jesus, the man you're looking for was crucified. But he is not here."

For a brief moment, there was a look of alarm on the faces of the women. "Where is he?" they cried with alarm. "What happened to him?"

The angel went on, "Oh, don't be alarmed. He is risen just like he said he would be. You may come and see where he was buried if you like. Then you must go quickly and give this message to his disciples. Tell them he has risen and will see them in Galilee as he had told them. There, I have given you the message I was supposed to."

The women were really confused now. On the one hand they were afraid because the tomb was empty, and on the other hand they were joyous that Jesus was raised from the dead. They were shocked suddenly when they heard the voice of Jesus behind them.

"Greetings," he said. They turned and knelt to worship him, and as they touched his feet he said, "Don't be afraid. Please go tell my brothers I will be in Galilee where they can see me."

The women hurried away to share the good news with his friends. Some of the guards went to the city and reported to the chief priest what had happened. Now the religious leaders really had a problem on their hands.

They had solved their first problem with money by paying Judas to betray Jesus. They solved their second problem by having Jesus crucified. They thought they would solve this third problem with money, too. They shared the plan with the soldiers. "Here's the story you're to report to the authorities. Tell them the disciples of Jesus came and stole him while you were asleep."

The soldiers were not immediately convinced that this was a good idea. But it's amazing what money can do. When the soldiers saw how much the religious leaders were willing to pay, they had a change of heart. But they had one more issue to deal with. They said to the men,

"What happens if this story gets to the governor? We could be in real trouble. We could even be executed for going to sleep on duty!"

"Don't worry about the governor," the religious leaders replied. "We'll keep him satisfied. You just stick to your story."

That is the official story told in Jerusalem to this very day.

When it was time, the eleven of us went to the mountain in Galilee where Jesus had told us to meet him. We saw him and worshiped him. But some still doubted.

Then, Jesus gave us his final message, "All authority in heaven and on earth is mine. It was given to me by my Father. You are to go and make disciples in every nation. Baptize them in the name of the Father, and of the Son, and of the Holy Spirit. Teach them to obey the commandments I have given to you. I will always be with you to the end of the world."

This is the end of my story. I had the amazing privilege of knowing Jesus as one of his special friends, and it changed my life forever.

Matthew